The Grand Scheme of Things
Stories

Small Harbor Publishing

The Grand Scheme of Things

For permissions and information on ordering books, contact
operations@smallharborpublishing.com.

Cover art: Megan Merchant, "I Woke to the Sound of Rain"
Cover design: Diana Baltag
Interior design: Claire Eder
Publisher: Allison Blevins
Director: Kristiane Weeks-Rogers
Managing Editor: Bianca Dagostino

THE GRAND SCHEME OF THINGS
SARAH CEDEÑO
ISBN 978-1-957248-53-0
Harbor Editions,
an imprint of Small Harbor Publishing

The Grand Scheme of Things

Sarah Cedeño

Harbor Editions
Small Harbor Publishing

for my beautiful boys and my wild family, with love

Contents

The Wash / 5

Professor Bird / 13

House, History / 23

Pooter from Church Street, circa 1990 / 33

You Hear Night Sounds / 35

What We Do Here on Earth / 43

Where To? / 53

Dear Victor, If I Could Write You a Letter / 63

Orient Express / 71

Bittersweet Nightshade and Other Childhood Influences / 79

Primal / 85

Cold Storage / 95

The Grand Scheme of Things

Nobody knew the sober, victorious feeling she had sometimes, when she knew how much she was on her own.

—Alice Munro

The Wash

The day it happened, I was hanging the wash: Rusty's and Robert's work pants, worn at the knees, shirts worn at the elbows. Their clothes had become the same size.

When the noon siren roared, I figured Rusty and his friend Timothy would paddle their large, wet feet up the middle of Borden Street for lunch, like always. Shortly after them would be Dakota, our tenant's wild pup, who'd been trailing along after the two boys all summer.

Instead, that day, Timothy York came with the police. They called after Timothy to wait, to let them explain, but he'd already smacked into me on his way up the porch steps and was crying. And breathless. And dripping with water—or was it sweat?

"It's Rusty," Timothy said. Then he said, "I tried." Timothy was a good boy who smelled like sour milk, and I suppose something about him gave off an air of safety.

When the police took over, a stern, scripted telling, I imagined the scene, put myself there with Rusty like a game piece. I always imagined what he was doing when I wasn't around. Even after—especially after—when I wanted to share in his death. The officers followed me down Borden Street to the bank of the canal, where they'd begin dragging soon.

I had imagined a group of onlookers clumped to the side, a neighbor trying to get Rusty's life back, rolling him over like a stone.

But that wasn't how it was. We stood at the long strands of grass by the canal, which had a slow perpetual force behind it, yet seemed still, as though nothing had happened there. Rusty was somewhere in the canal, waiting to be pulled out.

"What are you all looking at?" I yelled at my neighbors, who stood on their stoops or pretended to fuss with their gardens. "It could have

5

been any one of our boys. Rusty knows how to swim. He's fourteen!" I didn't have to explain my wailing.

The officers drove me to the station, where I waited until my husband came. They offered me a Coca-Cola, and maybe water crackers, or—yes—a cold cut sandwich, ham falling out like a long cool tongue.

Robert showed up when they offered me a drink, and I said, "I need to get to my son. He needs to come for lunch." I know this because Robert reminded me later, and often, what silly things came out of my mouth, a mirror making me smaller than I was.

When they pulled Rusty out later that afternoon, it wasn't a quiet thing. People were everywhere, like worms after a hard rain. How Robert heard, we'd never gone over. It didn't matter, even now, though the curiosity was there, how Robert had learned about our drowned child.

They parted for me to kneel by Rusty.

He was soaked through.

He didn't look like my son, but larger than life, and that's how he would stay in my memory. The easy smile had been erased from above his chin, baby-like with bloat. His lips had no feathering, his freckles had disappeared. He was nearly grey. He could have been sleeping, but his blood was a standing pool in his veins. There was no current, no wave. I willed him to move, but nothing made a move in him. I couldn't believe he was the boy I'd just seen that morning.

"No," I said to him like I had countless times. He was there, but he wasn't. Seeing him like that made every moment I hadn't spent watching him a waste.

Timothy's small voice was the only sound while I examined Rusty's face, the crease of his eyes, his shorts still soggy with canal water. It was unnatural to hear a young man's voice while I stared at my dead son.

"I'm sorry, Mrs. Bookliss," he said. His mother, a pretty, red-haired woman I'd never spoken to, stood behind him with her hand on his shoulder to hold him back, as though the tragedy were contagious. I wanted to hug Timothy, the last person Rusty had seen—and a hard thing to admit, but closer to Rusty, that summer, than I had been. My Rusty, who I always tried to hold back, had broken the chain.

Dakota ran over to Timothy, licked his knee, nudged his hand, and Timothy said, "Dakota. No. Haven't you done enough?" The boy began to cry. "It was his fault, Mrs. Bookliss! Dakota drowned him." As if it had only been the two of us, Timothy and I, who wanted someone to blame for losing Rusty.

Rusty had told me stories of Louis, Dakota's owner, the best builder at the Civilian Conservation Corps, how straight and fast his frames went up. Rusty had become his apprentice. To Rusty, the dog was the only thing better than Louis. A poor government camp-worker with a dog.

In the newspapers, Louis called Dakota "a mongrel, a playful puppy," as though the town might feel for the dog. According to Timothy, Dakota jumped in after the boys, playfully putting his paws on Rusty's shoulders, and then his back, and then any part he could get his paws on, as though the mutt, himself, needed to stay afloat.

In dreams to come, Dakota would howl on the bank of the canal with someone's hand holding his collar, telling him it's all right.

How had the puppy come here? How had Dakota made his way from across the country to this street, where Rusty grinned, his hair curling in the humidity, and then, that very minute against all other minutes, almost like an appointment, as though my whole life had been orchestrated for a moment I wasn't even present for, when Dakota managed to push him down in the canal, this trench dug so long ago, just a block away, where my grandparents just happened to move, in a town where the dog would happen to trot in, to root his residency, to jump in, to paw on a swimmer, my son, and why couldn't Rusty have just played baseball instead? The story could and would never make sense. The facts were not facts, but only circumstance, and now just some speck of history to be recounted in a trial. In the grand scheme of things, we are all harbingers of something.

I couldn't look at Louis, just seven years older than Rusty. He was somebody's son. All I wanted was my son—the dirt on his skin, a hair left on his pillow, evidence he'd once been here.

"Return my son," I yelled once toward the backyard of our rental property, where Dakota was chained to a stake in the yard. Dakota jumped up from his nap with his tongue showing itself and wagged his tail, pumped his paws. The dirt rose up around him.

The town had begun the trial. I went every day to the courthouse at first, and it was more a circus than anything else, with the dog in the courtroom.

Paramount Pictures sat at the edge of the proceedings that fall, a few men with hats and suits and cameras off in the corner, filming the dog. The town had never seen anything like it. I couldn't watch the men with the cameras, but Robert never stopped watching them.

When Louis took the stand, he argued, of course, that the dog hadn't known any better, that Rusty and Dakota spent a lot of time together. That Louis, himself, loved Rusty like a younger brother. He'd cried.

Looking back, it seems a horrific spectacle to mark the end of my son's life. There'd been no quiet moment to have lost a son. I went from having a perfectly healthy son to living in a prism of dog and judge and cameras, a place that never would have made sense had it been presented in a premonition. Dakota was on the cover of *The Republic*, where Rusty should have been. Images of the dog cradled in Louis's arms like his very own child. Both dog and Louis looked lovable, maybe misunderstood, but there was no understanding to be had, in my mind. This was it, I thought, what caused the outpouring from my own community in support of Dakota.

Hollywood outfits had offered Dakota roles in the movies. Something my son might have paid to see at one time. I began to stay home, sending Robert, alone, to watch the proceedings.

I smoked the butt-ends of Robert's cigarettes after he left. I'd move the flour and sugar in the cupboard to find Robert's whiskey and swish it between my teeth and cheeks, and after, finish what was left of the coffee. Every morning, I crossed the street to Louis's yard, plucking the ripe berries for breakfast, something I'd done since I was a child. This was how I went on.

When I needed groceries, I couldn't avoid the public eye any longer, and found people were equally frightened to see me, a scar they held the burden of mending. Robert wished I'd go to church with him, said the congregation looked at him as though he had a lazy eye. One day, I went to Clancy's to get the essentials: laundry soap, a steak, ham, bread, and potatoes. Neither Robert nor I wanted to eat.

I bought the steak for the dog. I crushed the nightshade that spiraled around the lattice next to the clothesline with mushrooms that sprouted in the humid rain, mixed them with oil and let the steak marinate overnight. I'd warned Rusty about nightshade, a berried vine that grew everywhere in the village and killed a young boy who'd eaten a handful.

The next morning, with Louis at the courthouse, and the dog left home, I snuck into the yard of the boarding property. I held the piece of raw meat in front of Dakota, who whined and tugged away from the stake he was chained to. I pushed the meat toward his muzzle and pulled it away, and then did that again. Each time I brought it closer to his nose, I pulled it back faster until, focused, he bit at it, and when I tugged at the other end, let go. He lay down and looked up at me like I was a fool. So I left it there, at his feet, and by the time I went to bed that night, I'd forgotten all about it. When I woke the next morning, the dog was still there, alive, and worse, the court had decided Dakota only be housebound for two years. In the rental property we owned.

Robert suggested Dakota be kept in a home outside of the village limits. But no, Judge Raymond argued, "That had no matter in the case."

"If I had a gun, I'd shoot that dog myself," I said at the close of the trial. Robert pinched my side and told me to shut up.

"She meant to say the ruling doesn't suit us," Robert said.

Looking back, I can't believe Louis would have stayed across the street from us, that he felt safe with me watching the dog.

After the court decision, I wanted to move. My gut fell every time I walked up to the house Rusty had painted with his skinny arms. But Robert didn't want to leave. And then Robert wanted to move. And I didn't. And we went back and forth this way until we realized that tug each other was all we had done this whole time and decided to leave each other alone, the way God had left each of us, and I felt sad for Robert he hadn't realized that yet.

Robert let Louis and Dakota stay in the apartment across the street since neither one of us had the energy to fight anymore.

From the windows, I watched Louis insist on living his life. As time passed, and Louis gathered his mail or carried a bag from the market into his house, or walked a young woman down the street, I began to look forward to his hold on life. When Louis kissed a girl on the lawn in broad daylight, I gasped, and when, at one time, I would have prayed, I made myself a tomato sandwich. Then I stared at the sun and felt much the way I had when I looked at Rusty becoming a man, something so bright it could scar my eyes. Had he ever left on his own, it might have seemed like he was punishing me for something I'd done wrong. By then, I'd made up my mind. Rusty had been too good for this world.

Though I didn't expect it, life after came back in its own way. On the bad days, my life hardly felt like the sun rose at all. Normal days woke slowly, but woke nonetheless, like the village in the morning—the milk trucks, the barber, post office and diner, the train on its route through town, until eventually, at midday, it was already business as usual and the sleep was gone from its eyes. Though when the sun went down, I would still be waiting for something to happen that had not.

After almost one year of being holed up, Dakota was freed early, pardoned by the Judge on National Dog Day. Of all things. A punchline where there should be none.

Lately, Louis offers help as though he can mend all this, so I let him do things around the house. Sometimes I give him tasks I expect to be impossible, just to see. He approaches as though I am a dog he doesn't trust, carefully and calmly. Business-like. Once I asked him if he could level my dining room floor. He went to the basement for a few hours, came back up, poured a half a glass of water on the planked floor and it pooled, but hardly moved an inch beyond. I couldn't even believe he'd done anything, but it was fixed. There were certain things I used to believe could never happen, though, and now I know better, that when the impossible happens, you must accept it. Even if it runs like a spectacle around in your brain, or sits like coal in your stomach, or severs the legs you once used to stand.

Today, after hanging the wash, I do what I should. While I pick raspberries, Louis walks out the door, and I tell him I want to make a supper I know he'll like, I can see he's thinning too much and needs a good meal, and I bet he can fit in Rusty's clothes, almost. He has become that small.

So he says, "Yes, sure," but has errands to run and disappears for a while. While he's gone, I boil the potatoes and fix the ham because if I don't, I'm worried he's not going to come back, that I've scared him away. Believe it or not, I wish I'd offered Dakota a spot on the floor beneath my kitchen table just to make sure Louis knows he's welcome, he knows he can come for dinner, and I'm thankful for him fixing my dining room floor. Life can sometimes be this simple, I want to say.

The cigarette I smoke while waiting for him to come back lights a fire in my lungs, a part of my body I once took for granted, when it had been possible to take things for granted. I can't even care if the clerk at Scranton's Market smirks at me when I ask for a pack of Chesterfields. This is how much I have left to lose.

When Louis comes back, I peer from behind the curtain of the living room window. What I see is enough to know Louis won't be coming for dinner.

Louis carries Dakota in his arms and the dog's head is hung so he's either hurt badly or there's not enough life in him to feel a thing. Just after Rusty died, I'd thought this dog, lifeless, would bring me peace.

I watch Louis cross the road, carrying Dakota to the yard behind his rental, where he lets the dog's body fall in a thud to the earth. I pace in front of the door to keep myself from heading to Louis.

I butter the potatoes before they get cold and put them in the oven.

From the door, I can see Louis with his head buried in his hands.

"Louis!" I call, pretending I don't know what I've witnessed as I leave my house.

"I can't come tonight after all," he says.

I ignore that, pretending I didn't hear.

"Well, supper's finished. Am I going to eat alone?" When I reach the gate to the yard, it's open and Louis sits on the ground next to the dog's body.

"Oh," I say. "Louis. I'm sorry," feeling foolish because I know what happened, and still am here, making a farce.

"It's all right, Mabel."

Louis stands up, fidgets with the lumber from the shed he'd been working on and ignores the body.

"You can't just pretend it isn't there," I say. "Is he…?"

"Dead. Someone saw him on the road," he says. "I'll bury him when I'm ready."

"You'll never be ready," I say.

"There have been worse things in my life that have happened to me than this, Mabel. It's a shame, it is. But it isn't the end of everything," he says, nailing what looks like any scrap of wood any old way on a frame that already seems sturdy to me.

"Perhaps not," I say. "Do you pray, ever?"

"I used to," he says.

"And then you realized it didn't help any?"

"No. I just tired of working at it when I wasn't sure if there would ever be an outcome," he says.

"There's always an outcome whether you pray or not. If something doesn't happen, nothing does. Sometimes that's worse."

"Want a cigarette?" Louis asks. I look at Dakota, unsure where the trauma is on his body. He's smaller than I remember him. The size of a pile of clothes I could carry in my arms. His mouth hangs open, as do his eyes, softer than I want them to appear.

"Yes," I say.

Louis lights the cigarette and passes it to me. I close my eyes while I let the stale air out.

He stares away from Dakota's body, and we sit, smoking, taking life in like gluttons. It's forbidden, this kind of breath, like we're children and we're soaking up the water and the sun and cigarettes like they are meant only for us.

Louis lets the air out in large rings, like halos.

I laugh.

"Taught Rusty how to do that," Louis says.

My heart doesn't know what to do with his name. I don't hear others speak it anymore.

Louis apologizes, but there's nothing he can say that makes what happened any more wrong, so I tell him he can't be sorry for saying what's true.

The rings float up and away. When we can't see them in the air anymore, Louis picks up a shovel and breaks the ground.

Professor Bird

The first time the professor and student sat together at The Cellar in the booth with the large "Draft Beer, Not Boys" poster hanging above it, Lottie wasn't sure why she'd gone. They drank the college bar's two-for-one happy hour special. They picked at the free popcorn, stale with the afternoon settling over it. Of course, Bird asked her how she was "liking" his class, suggesting she did.

"I like it fine," Lottie said. She didn't want to talk about his class but would humor him anyway. "Are we as good as other classes you've had?"

Bird reminded Lottie of the greyhounds her American Lit professor walked around campus. His leather band did nothing to keep his watch in place and it slipped up and down his arm each time he lifted the beer to his mouth. Maybe the delicateness of his frame captivated Lottie. Maybe it was his strange face shape.

"Talent's always about the same," Bird said. "Some students will improve, some will not. And then the semester's over." This answer satisfied Lottie, not necessarily because it was an adequate answer to her question, but because it made her feel like an exception, as if she'd transcended the student/professor barrier. She'd spent so much of her adolescence being told what she couldn't do: stay out past nine, be absent from school when she had bronchitis, play softball in middle school, listen to the Beatles, loudly, on repeat, play percussion, or join the high school debate team. When she grew older, maybe the age of twelve, she'd become a hassle, and her parents confirmed this through their nicotine haze and from behind their evening programs.

"You know," Lottie said, "I really love this psychology class I'm taking with Dr. Williams. He's so smart." Bird stared off toward the girls' bathroom as she said this and when he turned to her, he frowned.

"Dr. Williams, huh?"

She felt an instant elevation. Success. "Yeah. He just won this major research grant, I guess. He announced it in lecture." He hadn't.

Lottie asked Bird about her roommate Tamara's poem, "Love and Coat Hangers." Tamara was newly pregnant and frightened. No one understood the coat hanger part but Lottie—not the education students or literature students.

"Oh, it was juvenile," Bird said. "Nothing new, really."

Lottie felt herself blush, but also felt privileged to know what Tamara's poem was about, to understand the world in a way Bird didn't. And couldn't. Between Lottie and Tamara, Lottie hadn't expected it would be her roommate in this predicament. Some students became campus stars, leading protest rallies or publishing op-eds in the college newspaper to acclaim. And some dropped out and were drafted. Lottie and Tamara were bystanders.

Yesterday, after they'd discussed Tamara's poem in Professor Bird's class, Tamara asked Lottie for help. She was fixed on something their classmate mentioned to take care of the pregnancy. Lottie agreed. The two girls went to the hardware store to buy Vi-Jon's Turpentine, and after they'd concocted a cloudy yellow mixture, Tamara puckered just holding the tonic to her nose. Lottie suggested she cut the tonic with Tang and drink twice as much. So, she did.

"How about Silv's poem?" Lottie asked Bird. Silv thought she was the smartest because she always had a battle to fight. And because Silv organized a successful copycat bra burning in the campus mall, it sparked an instinct of competition in Lottie.

"I liked Silv's poem from last week," Bird said. "About fear of flying."

"Oh," Lottie said. *Was that what it was supposed to be about? Huh.* Lottie had thought it was about drugs.

She wasn't sure she even wanted to write poetry. She didn't want to write at all if she wasn't any good and shouldn't waste her time anyway. One semester was low stakes. Later, Bird would ask her what she wanted, and though they would be about to fall into bed, she would be confused by what he meant, and the question would follow her around for days.

But Bird encouraged Lottie as much as he did anyone else.

In fact, moments later, he placed his hand on hers over the table in their booth and said to her, "I couldn't get over your last poem about the dog, so I read it again and again. The images are disgusting and beautiful —what was it you said?—'Shards of flesh and sinew of bone'—but it needs some more contextualization, at least one more abstraction to give the carcass of the dog on the threshold some emotional resonance."

Brilliant, she thought. But she didn't understand any of what he'd just said and wondered if he even understood.

Bird's face was flushed and his eyes glassy. Earlier, he mentioned to the class his wife would be away for weeks, caring for her ill mother, and, today, when Bird offered to walk Lottie to her boarding house, just three blocks away, after leaving The Cellar without tipping, it ended as it would on many occasions after—not at her boarding house at all.

Bird shifted his attention from Lottie and called to a petite girl Lottie didn't recognize, "Laura! Hiya, honey." He put his arm around the girl— *Laura, honey!* She was pretty with black hair and green eyes and could have been Lottie's age.

"I was just having a conversation with one of my students about the final project."

Lottie bit down on a kernel. Sure. The final project.

"I'll see you at home," Laura said. "What time will you be there?"

"An hour or so," Bird said.

Lottie's head began to ache as the girl kissed Bird on the cheek and walked away. The more Lottie stared at her, the more she looked like a kid.

"That was my daughter," Bird said.

"She's beautiful. Why didn't you introduce me?"

"Just in case."

"In case of what?" Lottie asked. She pushed the popcorn toward him and took a last sip of beer.

"In case of anything," Bird said.

Everything was easier unnamed, Lottie understood. And she also knew, when two hours passed, and Bird still hadn't pulled his Volvo into the driveway but lay naked and passed out at The University Inn with Lottie's leg draped over his, Laura would find excuses for why her father was late because no one ever wanted to face a hard truth.

As the semester neared a close, Lottie remained shy about what would happen when Bird closed his bedroom door. He hung his necktie over the doorknob, where Lottie expected he never left it when his wife was home.

He liked it to seem as though having sex just *happened*, it wasn't planned, even though it was a regular thing after class on Tuesdays and Thursdays.

By this time, Lottie purchased her own stash of Nunbetters from Hazel's Drugs out of fear for herself and placed them on Bird's bedside table. Tamara was wrecked by the pregnancy, worried worse when it seemed nothing came of the Vi-Jon's tonic, and left Bridgeport early to explain her situation to her parents. Her friend could still button her pants, but Lottie noticed a general thickening about her, if it wasn't her imagination. Before she'd left, the two pushed their twin beds next to each other so Lottie could comfort Tamara. In the moonlight, Tamara lifted her wide face, the space between her front teeth almost large enough for another tooth, and then fell asleep with her head on Lottie's shoulder.

Lottie heard Bird's shoes come off, and then he yawned and stretched. She even knew enough not to yawn in class.

On the wall hung a close-up of Bird's wife amidst exotic tchotchkes from their travels—Italian masks, something Asian, and a bright woven textile Lottie couldn't help but notice. It was another world in front of her. Bird's daughter was the spitting image of his wife. Lottie wondered what his wife's name was and nonchalantly lay her head on a pillow and sniffed to see if she could smell her lotions or shampoo—she didn't seem the type for perfume. Though she knew she'd never get the chance to do it, Lottie wanted to rummage through her dresser drawers.

"What's your wife's name?" Lottie asked.

"Why do you want to know?"

"Just curious." She stood up and stepped closer to the photo, noticing a birthmark on his wife's cheek.

"She's a good woman," Bird said, stepping over. He and Lottie stood there, together, looking at her photo.

He seemed to love his wife. But then here was this. Lottie had never been in love before. This couldn't be love. Or, at least, she hoped love didn't feel like this. Her feelings for Bird came up as suddenly as the deer in the yard of her boarding house, completely unexpected, but recognizably captivating. Though when Lottie spent too long examining her lust for Bird, it startled off into the woods, and worse, when they slept together, any feelings for Bird long disappeared. She didn't know how to feel about the fact she didn't want to have sex with him. Occasionally, his musty black pepper scent repulsed her.

He still had his corduroys on—the same pair of corduroys he wore every day, it seemed. Or perhaps behind the other closet door sat multiple pairs of the same tan corduroys stacked neatly on the shelf.

The small sounds caused by Bird, but not actually his body (the unlovable grunts and sighs)—the knock of his watch against the dresser or the clink of his belt buckle on the hardwood floor and the slump of the corduroy—those were the disembodied noises Lottie lingered on, feeling eerie, vacant.

She endured it until the end, and just before, when she caught a glimpse of his blotchy face, Lottie felt pity for him, a need to tell him that whatever it was—his wife, his job—it would be okay. But what did she know? Sometimes he looked as though he was in pain or on the verge of tears with his crinkled lids or half-open mouth. Though she wanted to tell him it would be okay, she didn't because she knew better, and so she passed the time before Bird finished looking at his alarm clock, watching the spindly hands circle the Big Ben, waiting for the bell to ring out, and imagined him flitting out of her. But the alarm never sounded—he had no reason to set an alarm, no fear or urgency. When it was all said and done, his face became suddenly relieved, almost childlike. And after it was over, she felt a sense of pleasure and power for withholding her nurturing.

"My wife is coming home next month at the latest," Bird said. He explained classes ended before that, though, and his wife expected him to visit her in Ohio, where her mother lived, bedridden, as soon as school let out.

"Unless your mother-in-law dies sooner?" Lottie asked. The doctors gave her an expiration date, made something as complicated as Alzheimer's a matter of numbers and letters, but Lottie tried to think of it in simpler terms. The end of this thing she and Bird were doing.

"We should end this once the semester's over," Lottie said, testing him.

"Why would you want to do that?" His face seemed pleading, but his voice was sure, as though he'd recited it. "We don't have to end anything."

Bird didn't try much to hide what they were doing from others, and it seemed to Lottie he might expect his wife was doing much the same thing in Ohio.

That day, Bird explained that if he and Lottie tried to hide it, it would become a scandal, and for now, others around them took it as nothing, just a professor and student thing. When he'd said this, it infuriated Lottie. Not just because he thought she was nothing, but because it seemed he cared so little for what he had—his wife, his daughter—by sleeping with her. He risked nothing for nothing.

After he cleaned up and she cleaned up, Lottie said, "'A professor and student thing.' You know, you are a cliché."

"Perhaps," Bird said. He didn't care, and Lottie wondered what she could say to offend him. If she flicked him between the eyes, he wouldn't flinch, she thought.

Bird left for Ohio the day after grades came out. He gave Lottie a B. A B —the least committal of grades, and the more she thought about it, the angrier she became. It seemed less about her poetry and more about Bird's disappointment in his own life. As though he were unhappy in general and punishing her. So typical, and when she read the letter B, she swore she smelled her parents' ambivalence from their living room.

While Bird was gone, Lottie spent a strange amount of time at her boarding house, writing. She knew enough about poetry to know what bad poetry was and threw most of it away.

Maybe the amount of time she spent in the room she'd shared with Tamara, or more-so, the fact that Tamara was suddenly absent, made Lottie long for her childlike wholesomeness—someone she easily could have become.

Tamara wrote Lottie letters while she was away. Her pregnant friend had grown so much she could no longer ignore her pregnancy, and she became more and more scared about giving birth. Tamara's mother was awful to her, telling her she would take the baby after her birth and give it up for adoption—Tamara would be a terrible mother. Tamara took another dose of Vi-Jon's and Tang, and by the next time Lottie heard from her, she'd miscarried. She'd spent days in the hospital, and Lottie didn't know if from the miscarriage or from poisoning herself, too. Once she lost the baby, Tamara's voice became more frantic. What Tamara meant was to gain relief, Lottie thought. But she lost the baby as expected, and the absence lingered in her body.

"I need a favor," Tamara said over the phone one night, and Lottie worried from the terrible result of the last time she'd helped Tamara.

"Anything," Lottie said. And then she couldn't back down. Lottie had cried over Tamara's loss when she told her the horrifying details, huge wilting blossoms in toilet water, an image Bird might have underlined in a poem but not understood. She felt partly responsible because she'd helped her concoct the tonic, and now, responsible for helping pick up the pieces. Tamara might have been at home with her mother, but she explained to Lottie she felt entirely alone, and so Lottie understood the assignment.

"Will you confess at St. Agnes?" Tamara asked.

"What? If I confess for you, it doesn't absolve *you* of anything."

"I won't ever be absolved, but I need to know what the Father will say, and he can't know what *I've* done. I've heard awful things. I'm going to Hell," Tamara said. "Will you confess to aborting? Tell me what he says?"

"I'll go," Lottie said. She told Tamara any God worth worshipping forgave. Whenever religion entered part of an analysis in literature classes, Lottie nearly broke out in hives. It was the one time she kept her mouth shut because she knew nothing at all. She'd only been in a Catholic church once that she could remember—at her grandmother's funeral service. At first, the church felt warm to her but grew chilly when everyone else knew exactly what to do and she did not.

Bird had a cross in his living room. He'd been an altar boy and described himself as a lapsed Catholic, though Lottie had heard him mention going to campus mass on occasion.

Over the phone, Tamara instructed Lottie the right words to say, becoming eerily calm:

"Praise be Jesus Christ," Tamara enunciated. Lottie tried not to think much about the words she copied down.

They kept going like this, back and forth, Tamara listing what the Father, in turn, would say until what Lottie had written down resembled a script.

The chapel air rang stale, and Lottie worried she'd be discovered a fraud, confessing Tamara's sins and leaving out her own.

There wasn't the line she would have expected for confessions on a college campus. Lottie sat in the booth and spoke the words she had written down on a piece of paper the night before.

"For ever and ever. Amen," the Father said. Lottie was disappointed the Father's voice wasn't sterner. And wasn't he a Priest? Tamara said 'Father.' And what was the difference? What business did she have here, not knowing who she spoke to?

Lottie grew nervous, of course, during the listing of Tamara's sins, a few of which she, herself, was guilty of.

"Bless me Father, for I have sinned. It has been six months since my last confession. I have lied many times, to many people, including my parents. I have had sex out of wedlock a number of times I cannot count. I have tried twice to abort a pregnancy, and once to take my life. I have aborted a pregnancy."

Lottie read the list many times the night before. She'd have images of the handwritten words imprinted in her mind forever. The Father was silent, perhaps shocked. And then Lottie spoke again, words not on the paper. Her stomach cycled as she thought of Bird's wife and daughter.

"I had sex with a married man." She thought quickly, not carefully. "You probably know Professor Bird from the English Department. He's my instructor. Catholic, too. I have looked his daughter in the eye and smiled." She hoped the Father knew him, hoped he would corner and shame him for this.

"Does he know you've aborted his child? You should tell him."

Oh, Lottie thought.

When he spoke, he seemed calm enough. He didn't say either of them would go to Hell, but she couldn't really have imagined the Father would tell the truth if they were really doomed to Hell.

On the way home, Lottie worried about having to tell Tamara she would be excommunicated because of the tonic, but considered she might not tell her. There was no form to fill out, and so, really, it could all disappear. As she walked, she counted ten couples holding hands or hugging. One couple made out on the front steps of Heddon Hall. She imagined Tamara saw pregnant women all around her, happily rubbing their bellies because life pokes us right in the eye.

Bird called Lottie one last time while his wife was out. It was after he'd buried his mother-in-law. There were loads of sympathy cards scattered open like scissors around the house, and funeral bouquets wilted in vases. Bird was tanner and grayer, evidence of a life that kept on when Lottie wasn't around. Lottie already made up her mind to end it, but didn't have the chance because Bird ended it first.

"What time was her appointment?" Lottie asked, looking out the window. She'd never been there while his wife was in town. The house smelled different, maybe it was the flowers, maybe it was his wife.

"I just wanted to say bye," Bird said.

His eyes were swollen and red as though he'd had a tough time in Ohio, and when he hugged her, he smelled like beer. She let him kiss her. Bird was as horrible at ending relationships as he was at maintaining them. They said goodbye, and Lottie felt something lift in her.

The front door opened before Lottie made it out. Bird's wife was on the other side, looking better than Bird did. She was smaller than she appeared in the photographs. But of course, her features were familiar, down to the birthmark.

Lottie had never felt so far away. And from where, she didn't know. It was like coasting alone somewhere, above the ground. But then Bird's wife hugged Lottie. She smelled like marijuana and wine, and the sudden and strong way his wife held her made her realize she'd known nothing of him this whole time. Even still, now, Lottie called him by his last name. His wife felt like substance compared to Bird, as though he should be his wife's counterpart, instead of vice-versa.

"Lottie. Right?" his wife said as she left the embrace. She sounded sleepy.

"She was just leaving," Bird said.

"Why don't you stay awhile, Lottie? Why don't I tell you all the fun we had in Ohio, how our life is all paychecks and caviar dinners and dead parents and young, pretty college students." She turned to Bird. "Fuck off, Theodore."

Theodore? Lottie noted.

"Lottie, do you even know my name?"

She didn't and wished she did. Or at least wished Bird's wife would stop saying "Lottie."

Bird was standing with his back to them, and Lottie tried to imagine what his face looked like. His wife knew more about Lottie than Lottie knew about his wife. All Lottie could think was Bird must have confessed.

His wife turned to Lottie. "Do you have a clue what it's like to be forgotten? To have one person wipe you off the planet in their mind. He was sleeping with you while my mother forgot how to breathe."

Lottie hadn't spoken a word since she'd said 'Goodbye' to Bird. She couldn't have if she wanted to. Her mouth might as well have held a cup of sand. Lottie held tight to her tears and swallowed.

When Bird opened the door for Lottie, his wife threw her arm out as though to usher her into a faraway universe.

Lottie said, "Thank you," and walked carefully down the steps, unsure of what the hell she'd been thinking this whole time. She was sickening, a word reserved for putrid shame.

Sometimes it was impossible to avoid that house on her way through town—if the Birds even lived there anymore. When she did have to pass 87 Canal Street, beige with a portion jutted out like a princess tower, she was overcome by a suddenly sour stomach she carried for the rest of the day.

House, History

Madge and Paddy Wallace sat on their front porch in the rain, watching the Forbes' Tudor-style house turn the corner of Central Avenue.

At the opposite corner was as expected: the Our Lady of Mercy Church, and across the street, too, the Warrens' house and the post box sturdy as ever, but then there was the Forbes' house taking up much of the street. The bells from the tower of the newly minted Bridgeport State Teachers College had just rung out, and the church bells a block down would ring out any minute. The mail carrier delivered as normal, his cap shielding the rain as much as it could, and though it was pouring, he stopped to admire the Forbes' home amidst the chaos. The home looked like it would topple over, the peaked roofline outweighing the short side. Its customary brown timber outlines looked too simple, like lines in a coloring book. Paddy might not even believe it were real if he weren't sitting right there.

This was about college expansion. Tomorrow, Madge and Paddy's house would be demolished for college dormitories. Their house swept away—dinner crumbs from the evening table.

The owners of the fancy houses, like the Forbeses, "simply moved" to avoid the campus sprawl. But Madge and Paddy were advised not to move their modest Cape Cod, which might not withstand the move, anyway. Madge never lived any place else. Everything formative in her life happened there. If one looked at the home with some interest, it told a story of tragedy: the photos of her sister on the mantel from before the accident showed two little girls, Madge and Beatrice. Beatrice, frozen at the age of five, her hair bobbed, toes pointed like a ballerina's, the white smock and the grimace she wore from the sunshine.

Madge sipped the iced tea in her left hand and flicked the cigarette in her right.

"You all right?" Paddy asked.

"Our last night here, I guess. Let's set it on fire." Her hair was fuzzy with heat and rain.

"Gimme something to throw at them," Paddy said.

"They haven't done anything. They're just moving," Madge said. Moving meant packing boxes and leaving an empty house behind. The Forbeses weren't moving.

Some sparks in Madge surprised Paddy—like the time he walked into the bathroom to find her taking scissors haphazardly to her hair. Some things became commonplace. For instance, when Paddy, a chemist who taught at the college, came home from the lab to find Madge pressing her cheek to the kitchen table, her eyes fixed to an imaginary point on the horizon. As a result of misunderstanding her, he had a stock response and left her encouraging notes on recipe cards or lab paper— "You are my sunshine!" "This, too, shall pass!" At work, he read study after study about lithium, an element that could someday heal his wife. For now, Madge endured induced seizures via electroshock. Paddy was relieved not to have been allowed in the room because he felt it was a form of torture, deep down.

Their mouths grew thick with gin and the air soured from the little sun after the rain. The sky turned a putrid yellow-green and the traveling shadow from the Forbeses' house resembled the end of the world.

Paddy might have thought Madge was going to meet the mailman, to get the last of their mail postmarked at this address. Perhaps he thought she was getting a closer look through the Forbeses' windows—after all, a house in motion was on display. Maybe he thought she neared the road to grab one last glance at the crumbling bricks, the rotting pillars, the village's oldest rhododendron, to be plowed over the next morning. In hindsight, though, it seemed inevitable Madge would throw herself in front of the wheels of the flatbed truck.

It was a chaotic scene on its own, moving a house. Men flocked around the sides of the truck, holding their bare hands out for shelter as if to prevent it from falling off the flatbed. The house moved slowly. Slowly. And still, if it fell, there was no way around it—the men would be crushed. But the danger was irrelevant. The movers and spectators were so caught in the magic of a home changing addresses. The people involved became optimistic—anything could happen! Look at all that power! They didn't see Madge, and Paddy nearly didn't either. Madge had a miniature set of ribs and delicate arms and legs. She moved like a hummingbird through life—or in this case, through the front lawn. It was easy for her to be overlooked.

Moving a house was loud business. The men all shouted and whooped and hollered commands. *They were important!* And if Madge didn't want to be seen running to the truck, Paddy thought, she would have done it any way she could. He wished he'd seen it happening, her sneaking to the street.

Paddy was by her feet in time to see the truck lurch and the driver run to Madge, who lay absolutely still on the brick road, her short hair flicking in the breeze. Her body and her calm, tired face untouched. Paddy's arms and legs betrayed him—how encumbering a body could be. The house loomed behind the couple and the angry driver who Paddy recognized as the man who updated their inefficient windows one summer.

"What in the hell?" the driver shouted, hopping down from the truck.

Madge refused to move. Paddy picked her up.

"Put me down, Paddy!" she yelled.

Paddy considered setting her down.

"Keep her off the road," the man said. "I'll call the officers if not."

"Who the hell are you?" Madge shouted. Paddy decided to carry her back to the porch, arms and legs flailing.

"Madge! You can't run in front of a truck! Of all people, you know that," Paddy said.

It could happen in the fantasy world of the moveable homes. It could happen in the wake of church bells.

To start all this, last fall, Mayor Allen invited himself and his wife over for potluck dinner at Paddy and Madge's. The man was skinny with a kind smile, though Madge and Paddy knew this was how he operated: if a family were to be slighted, the mayor came to dinner, and he also brought his wife.

Paddy was the first to greet the older couple. Madge stayed in the kitchen tending dinner. She had a hunch, she'd read the papers, she'd known what it was about: the need for more classrooms and more housing for students. They were all, men and women, ready to enlist in a new sort of future after this last World War: education. There were houses and trees and a few businesses to be cleared to make way.

The slight mayor next to his tall wife made Paddy laugh, on the inside, of course: disproportionate, and everyone in town knew the position of Mayor was not actually held by Mr. Allen, but by his wife. She meant business. By the end of the meal, Madge would hate her.

"Well, Paddy, your wife was chubby as a little one, wasn't she? But sweet," the mayor's wife said after she entered the house, gesturing at Beatrice, Madge's twin sister.

The portrait had been there since Beatrice's death in 1935, Madge had told Paddy, and she wouldn't move the large frame no matter how hard it was to see it so many times in one day.

Every time the door opened upon entering the house, the natural light cast an angelic shine on Beatrice's already cherub-like face—her eyes were smiling and her chin, round as her cheeks.

Madge quietly appeared in the kitchen doorway. "If you thought long enough before speaking, Mrs. Allen, you might not assume it's me. That's my dead sister," Madge said.

Paddy kept moving, trying to take hats and talk about campus events —small talk meant inconsequential talk. Madge was all about consequences. When he turned around after saying something like, "Some storm last night," Paddy was stunned to see the faces of the two sisters side-by-side for the first time, staring at him. The framed Beatrice, innocent and wide-eyed on the short wall next to the kitchen opening, and Madge, eyes narrowed and frowning, her hands wringing a dishtowel.

Madge spoke again. "She was not chubby. She was beautiful. And four, in that picture."

The mayor's wife acted as though she hadn't heard a thing Madge said and grew a flat staunch smile for the rest of the evening.

And when the mayor informed Paddy and Madge, as a guest at their house, that their home would be bulldozed, he grew awkward and apologetic, maybe reverential at the loss, remembering how Beatrice's tragedy reverberated through the town for years. But his wife kept going.

"Paddy, a new chemical laboratory will be built just there." The mayor's wife pointed in the direction of the home's library. "You'll never be far from where your home was."

"You're going to put a science building over my father's library?" Madge raised her voice.

"No, far beyond—across that street there," Mayor Allen said, gesturing toward Utica Street, twisting his head like a confused dog. Paddy recognized an admirable and pitiable sense of hope in the man.

Madge kept her eyes focused on Mayor Allen's wife and pointed with her fork toward Mayor Allen. "You are a hard, horrible man, telling me my family home is being demolished so my husband can have a new laboratory to play with chemicals!"

After the mayor took his wife home, Madge broke some dishes, shattering one after another against the wood floor. The floor was littered with shards of china and smears of dinner.

Mashed potatoes, bits of chicken, the mayor's broccoli casserole, which Madge didn't touch.

No matter how Madge's episodes started, they always dissolved into Beatrice, a topic Paddy felt sludged in. There was no sense to be made from it. There was no getting around the swift end to Beatrice's life. Madge, just five at the time, watched it happen, she insisted, though her mother said Madge had actually been at her father's office getting an infected bee sting drained. Paddy imagined Madge then, where the slate walkway to her house met the town sidewalk, and her sister, lying in the street behind the milk truck, skull fractured, arms and legs broken. He'd read the death certificate. And Madge told Paddy about it so many times he felt like he'd been there, too.

Sometimes Paddy could hardly remember the days of their marriage at all—a smudged view from a passing train. After they married, Paddy moved into Madge's childhood home to help Madge care for her dying mother. Madge couldn't have been happier. For just a minute, Paddy saw peace in her forehead. Madge was all her mother had, after all.

Children were never so for the couple. They just never happened. Madge told Paddy once, having children meant you would never be alone.

Madge's mother passed on a yellow morning in the downstairs den-turned-bedroom in a way that let Madge feel as though she hadn't died at all, the single French door ajar, the house quiet except for the ticking of the clock in the family room. She slipped away so slowly, one thing after another, lights extinguishing one by one on a night street. The last sound she made sounded like a quiet giggle, and Madge smiled. Paddy told her a joke: "If you can't helium, and you can't curium, you might as well barium."

As the town hit dusk, the glow from the cigarettes speckled the porches on Central Avenue. The Forbes' house landed on the corner of Madison and Main in the Our Lady of Mercy Church yard until the next day, when the foundation would be ready at the home's new property. The earthmovers and tractors were already parked outside the house across the street, glaring at the couple, ready to push the home's bones around.

"This was never our house anyway," Madge said. Her words all began to blur together, and her mouth was bitter with gin.

"It wasn't?" Paddy asked.

"I haven't been a child in years," Madge said. "And this house wants children."

"Oh. Well," he said. "Well," and that was all he could think to say. He wasn't sure what he meant.

Madge drew so hard from her cigarette Paddy thought she'd turn cross-eyed.

"Look at the Tompkins family," he said. "Sure, they're able to move their house safely to a big lawn across from the Normal School, but they lost their four-year-old son. Once, you'd have thought they had it all, Madge. Now they have a big house and no son. Everything has a risk. Having children means you can lose them."

That wasn't the right thing to say, Paddy thought. Even if it was true. It didn't make any sense. Life didn't make any sense.

"You're right," Madge said. "That makes sense." She rested her head against the chipping porch post.

Paddy was a chemist and still, he had no idea about the alchemy between he and his wife. The acidity of Madge's thoughts combined with her sister's ghost bulged up like a clogged tube, obstructing her at every turn. She felt she had nowhere to go—especially now.

"Paddy," she said. Neither of them knew what came next.

Paddy put his arm around her. "This is just a house," he said.

Over the last months, they'd marched their lives from this house. First, the seasonal clothing items and boots they wouldn't need until the snow. Those left in trunks to the allocated warehouse along with cartons of books and photos. Then, the sofas, spare beds one and two, dressers and dishes and finally, all but the stark sets of silverware and hygiene items.

"I'm not leaving," she said. Paddy could feel she was serious, she wouldn't be able to leave. Her feet looked separate from her, dirty and elegant, tucked up on her chair, unaffected by emotion.

Paddy and Madge spent their last night on the floor of the room they once called their bedroom. Paddy wondered if there were any last-minute motions he could make to the mayor to save the home.

Through the open windows, Paddy could hear stray cats mating or calling out. Paddy and Madge kissed, tried to make love, but it was a clumsy moment and didn't work for either of them. College students walked by—out far past curfew—whooping and yelping and the careful kids, whispering.

The crickets chirped in their garden. Their wind chimes tick-tocked familiarly in the westerly breeze. Paddy had seen a lot of things, but never a house come down.

"What are you thinking about?" Paddy asked.

"My sister," Madge said.

Madge recalled bathing her twin sister, impossibly. Combing her light hair, feeding her, and teaching her how to talk all by herself. It was impossible she raised her sister, and still, Madge believed it to be true, and sometimes so much, Paddy began to believe it, too. Madge believed she'd been a mother her whole life.

That night Madge insisted everything around her would disappear and no one would remember her or Beatrice and before she knew it, it'd only be Paddy here, by himself, the only one with a name.

"How will my sister find me?" Madge asked.

Paddy knew this was in the back of Madge's mind the whole time, in this house—perhaps behind the wallpaper or in the putty between the wood planks, were the spirits of her family, declining in half-lives by time and space. "She's buried in the Hill Street Cemetery with your Ma and Pa," Paddy said. "We can still visit her grave."

"You know what I mean, Paddy," she said. "Her spirit is here. How will she know how to find me?"

He couldn't reason with Madge. She faced loss after loss. He was cotton worn thin, trying to intercept her from death. What could he do? Follow her everywhere, protecting her from herself? What if he failed, as he almost had that afternoon?

Unable to sleep, Paddy went out to the porch and sat where Madge had that afternoon.

There was an extra house on the street that night, and a candle or gaslight in the attic. The family had turned in. Tomorrow, the movers would pick it up like a suitcase and set it on its new foundation, and the doors would open and close as usual and the same people would sleep beneath its roof.

Paddy had seen it all.

The light in the attic at the Forbes' house went out. Paddy looked at his watch and then out at the sidewalk as though something would change.

In the morning, Madge and Paddy stared at the construction trucks and ate the only thing left in their freezer: apricot kolach, Madge's mother's recipe. Across the street, Mr. Forbes ran outside with a glass, laughing, and called to his neighbor for the day, Mr. Stevens, "You wouldn't believe it! This glass didn't spill a drop the whole move here."

"Well, isn't that something?" Madge asked Paddy under her breath, nudging him with her big toe. "Something to write home about—if you knew your own address!"

"If the damned house would only stay put!" Paddy said.

They tapped the tips of their cigarettes, sending ashes to their feet.

"Cheers," Paddy said.

The foreman came over to ask if Madge and Paddy would be watching, as a crowd of vaguely familiar faces accumulated in the street, but the couple said they'd be leaving shortly.

It was time. Paddy and Madge walked through the house, past the vacant wall where Beatrice had hung, through the empty kitchen and pantry, still hinting of spice and oil. Madge's mother's last breaths were long gone from the den, and the furniture she'd rested on, too. They'd left the blanket and their pillows on the hardwoods of their old bedroom. The Wallaces crept down to the basement, where Madge had canned last year. Her bare feet didn't make a sound in the moist dirt, still wet from yesterday's rain. Paddy led her to the crawl space below the living room and lay down with the cobwebs and spiders. Neither said a word.

Pooter from Church Street, circa 1990

Pooter was a chubby thumb of a toddler with a blond tail at his nape. He wore diapers exclusively and his baba never left his hand. His feet were calloused like puppy pads from the outdoors, and he had scabbed knees. Pooter lived in The Purple House.

The Purple House was occupied strictly by transients. Children ran in never-ending supply around the front yard turned patch of dirt. Pooter's was the only name anyone knew because that summer, he was always being scolded.

Pooter! Get back here, Pooter!

No one remembered seeing Pooter writing on cracked sidewalks near the train tracks, nor poking potato bugs with a stick until they curled into a tiny gray ball next to blades of grass. No one saw Pooter stomp on a hill of red ants next to the Pink Panther popsicle stick he dropped the day before. No one remembered Pooter with a blanket or a hot dog, ever. Nor rain boots nor a new bike and definitely not a Slip 'n Slide.

No one remembered Pooter's night terrors of unclear images like fire, or slaps, or muffled screaming. No one saw Pooter pick poison from the chain-link fence and pop the ripe rainbow berries into his mouth. No one remembered seeing Pooter play with the skinny Doberman the old man kept tied to the bumper of his car, towed when he was evicted. No one knew if Pooter visited the train tracks next to Stall's Hardware on the wrong side of Erie Avenue.

The Church Street kids liked Pooter even if they didn't know him. They hear his name in memories with stray cats and the hum of the Cold Storage in the dusty sunshine.

Dr. Mills, your landlord, pulls his truck into the stone driveway.

"What's that there?" he asks, as though you need to explain what it is rather than why it's on his front porch. He's a professor at SUNY Bridgeport, he should be smart enough to figure it out for himself.

There's a note tagged to the top of the cage.

"A turkey. His name is Darryl."

Darryl looks far stranger up close—as stunned as you are.

You read the note to the professor.

"James. Here is Darryl. Your father pisses himself every night. Eats nothing but potato chips. How can he raise a turkey? I saw you looking at Darryl before you left, like you said goodbye. He's yours now. Mom."

You hand it to him as proof, hoping your voice, tripping through the note, eases his response.

"Well. Suppose we'll have to keep him out back," Dr. Mills says. "I've got chicken wire hanging around in the barn. Fix it up for him to stay for now."

Maybe you've spoken to both of your parents for the last time, and you could offer Darryl to the Millses for a holiday meal. Then you wonder how your mother found the Millses' house.

Your parents live in another town, not a college town, but along the same canal as your boarding house. It's far enough away, you might forget your demented father, his missing history, the words and times and functions that have escaped him. Now, it's likely your father is on the back porch, alone, scratching his head. You wonder if you should have told the Millses your father was dying.

A few months ago, when your father came home from chasing ducks along the canal bank in your small town, he carried Darryl, the turkey a farmer gave him, to coax him from the canal. That night, you'd told your father something that surprised you even though you said it. Something you wish you could get away from.

"Sometimes I want to kill," you said. The back porch was the only place you and your father ever talked. Some days, he could barely remember your name, the child he'd once chased from fence to door, challenging you to run faster, try harder. Your adoptive parents (you don't have real parents) used to fight over who taught you things, each would point at the other and back away from you at the same time. You never learned to tie your sneakers.

"Kill what? A squirrel?" he asked. "I don't know how to hunt."

"With my hands. Anything that will stay put long enough," you said.

"Not a squirrel, then," he said.

You made sure—real sure—you believed his memory was tender and unfortunate like roadkill.

Then, you let it fly, "Like women," you said.

After, your father dove further into dementia, never recalling your name and only talking to you about Darryl.

Ever since your mother dropped Darryl off, Marty and Duke—the two assholes who board with you—call you Turk when they address you, which is hardly at all. They're the type of kids who call girls "baby" and get all the action.

Some days, when Darryl trills for an hour or two, the others in the house avoid you. Sometimes, in the evenings, when you go out to check on Darryl in the yard, Mrs. Mills—a fox if you ever saw one—comes to see you.

The sun shines over, through, and eventually, beneath the pines, so Mrs. Mills' skin speckles with sweat, and you try to focus on the turkey. Then, you say something peculiar, like, "Dinner was tasty," or "I wish my mother could cook like that," or "A guy could marry a woman who cooks a chicken like that," and she leaves to grab a few weeds from the garden's edge.

But tonight, something different happens.

"Your mother just called," Mrs. Mills says.

"Did she say what she wanted?"

"You should call her back now," she says, her eyes steady on Darryl. He has stopped carrying on but still flaps his wings every minute or so in frustration. "You have to call her back."

You both walk toward the house. You don't look at her. Once inside, you move toward the stairs like a child from punishment.

She steps in front of you and picks up the receiver, holding it out to you with her hand you want to hold and break at the same time

"I think you ought to call her right away," she says.

You don't talk.

"Dial," she says.

You dial.

Your mother's voice is tired or sore or less stupid.

"It's Jimmy," you tell her.

You pretend she doesn't say what she actually says, though your mind takes over, and you imagine your father, already a ghost, suspended in air, in the basement, from an electrical wire.

You ask your mother, "Are you relieved, too?"

She hangs up.

Mrs. Mills knew already, asks if you want to go home, if you need a ride from Dr. Mills.

"What's your first name?" you ask.

She doesn't answer, but again, offers a ride to your parents' house. Your mother's house.

"No," you say.

From outside their bedroom door, you hear the Millses arguing about you. Dr. Mills wants to force you to go home, and Mrs. Mills insists you are *not normal,* they should give you time.

You've had three dreams about Mrs. Mills since you've moved in, but when you see her in the house, it's not often you speak. You take the silence as a quiet bond. In a dream you can't get out of your mind, Mrs. Mills is small enough to lurk around your ankles, a mass of brown-red hair, and you only realize it's her when she skulks away.

Instead of going to your father's service, you sit by the canal with your camera and watch late-season boaters doing normal things: eating hot dogs, spilling beer overboard, posing for pictures they don't know are being taken. You tell yourself any section of the canal is like being home, but you know it's a lie. You imagine all the accidental drownings:

disappeared college students, a semester's time passed before they're really gone; a librarian or a hooker, late for her next shift; a professor's wife, a half-empty bed.

Saturday evening, you see Mrs. Mills setting food out for a feral cat in the yard and drop your book bag. The cat is a few feet away, an ugly thing, a whore of a cat. Mrs. Mills looks up at you, her head near your knees, and as you bend down to pick up the bag, you can smell the cold ground beef she's got in the cat bowl and feel ill.

She asks how you're doing.

"Fine," you say.

"How are classes?" she asks.

You've only gone to a few since they began, though you say, "Good." One of the house rules is you must be a student.

"Are you getting along with the boys?"

She means Marty and Duke, who you know would have thrown eggs at you in the high school locker room, too, were they there.

"Yeah. Okay," you say, though you barely talk to them. Except the other day, when whichever one of them asked, *Turk, why you taking pictures of the Millses' bed?*

The sheets were pushed back, the lumps cast hills on the bed. When you went downstairs without answering the boys, the couple was sipping coffee at the kitchen table. You hate coffee. You felt like you shouldn't have walked in.

"Okay, then. Where you heading?"

"Town," you say. "Catching a ride."

"Your mother called again tonight. Are you going to return her calls, Jimmy?"

"Sometime, maybe."

Walking away, you feel like you kept half the conversation still in your mind. When you look back, she's still holding out her hand with the bowl of ground meat in it.

You're supposed to cook one meal a month for the Millses and the boarders and need soy sauce for your mother's pork ball recipe, the only thing you know how to make.

The man who gives you a lift to town tells you about all the ghosts the canal holds. Then he continues to the next street, where the supermarket is. When he lets you off, he asks you for money.

"I don't have two nickels to rub together," you say, like your father.

He mutters something and pulls away with his middle finger in the air.

You give him two fingers back and yell, "Peace!" but feel stupid as soon as you let your hand drop.

In the market, you try to imagine the cashier you've just passed. Even when you talk to people, you stare, not past them or through them, how people say it happens, but worse—away from them, like the repulsion of magnets from each other.

Maybe the cashier's hair is long and brown; maybe she'd been on the phone with her boyfriend until early morning, maybe she will go missing and her boyfriend will head up a search committee, dredging the canal with his fingers, scraping the bottom until all he finds besides a tire or a grocery cart is a cow carcass.

In any other situation, she would not say 'hello' in response to your existence.

You spend some time in the hygiene aisle, near the toothbrushes and condoms, where the cashier would blush if she followed you. You might remember your only ex-girlfriend from high school, only skinnier, or even a nameless face, or maybe you'll look at the clerk and feel the heat in your waist.

One girl you took pictures of in high school never actually wrote the love letter some jock (might as well have been Marty or Duke), sporting a varsity letter, slipped into your locker with her name signed to it. You screwed up your locker combination so many times you thought it was part of the trick to mess up twice before it'd open. The paper fell out with perfume and lip stains on it.

You took the letter home, fantasized that as the girl's nails pressed against the hard barrel of the pencil, she mouthed the words. You'd stroked the paper, your mouth clumsy over each syllable, wrecking the romance before you even knew it was fake. You picture a group of guys spraying the samples from the cosmetics aisle on the lined paper. If you see them in that aisle, it won't matter because you're on different planes.

The cashier's drawer opens with a crash as coins slam against each other. She chats with another customer about last week's small-town drama—your crazy father's suicide—and when her fingers pull out the change, she's probably miscounted. She doesn't even know you're there.

You've stolen before.

There's dust on every label—the catsup, the mayonnaise, lamely and barely in rows, and no one has touched any of them in months. You shove your hands in your empty pockets, then pick up the jar of soy sauce with its thin dark liquid inside, ready to stash it in your book bag, and realize you left your bag in the truck.

As if you called for the man who dropped you off here, he's at the end of the aisle, like he'd left you right at that spot.

He says, "You left your bag. Thought about keeping it, but that's a nice camera you got in there."

You say, "Yeah. Thanks."

"I'm suspicious of weirdos, but I wouldn't steal from one. You need a ride back?"

"Sure," you say, and leave the soy sauce. It's getting dark.

He drives the main road back to the boarding house.

All at once: a crack, a thud. "Fuck," the driver says, and then a jerk and a halt.

"What the hell was that?" you ask.

"How do you like that?" he says. "A buck."

The driver is in front of the truck shaking his head at its hood, and you wonder what kind of a dipshit stands in front of his idling car with a killer in the cab. Then he looks behind the truck at the culprit.

In the rearview mirror, you see the buck, still, cockeyed in the middle of the road, one antler up. Pathetic little pisser.

"Get out," he says to you from the other side of the window. "Help me put this sucker in the back."

You get out. Even dead, its weight makes him more alive than you are. You wipe your hands on your pants and get in the car.

"That'll be dinner someday," he says. "Can't waste it."

"Yeah," you say.

He's moved the car to the shoulder now and takes something from the glove compartment in front of you.

"Want some?" he asks, lighting the short white stick.

"Yeah."

"Here," he says, holding it out to you like communion.

You suck hard. You've done this before. After seeing your father's stoned eyes, you found the boys who put bogus love letters in your locker, and, pretending it never happened, spent every cent you had on drugs before you came to college. You'd asked them for "marijuana," what your mother called it, and they said, "You mean a doobie? Some weed?"

You drank beers with them once, too, until they left the bonfire to go in the house and locked the door, left you pounding until you thought your fists would bleed.

Mrs. Mills won't lock the boarding house until after you're back. Her bedroom door doesn't have a lock either. You fill up your lungs, and when you can't take it anymore, open up, and cough the smoke out.

When the driver's pulled away from the shoulder, he says, "Want part of the buck?"

"No. I'm boarding," you say.

"Fine by me," he says.

There's a thud from the back.

"Shit. You hear that?" the driver asks.

"Yeah," you say.

"Son of a…" the driver looks up in his rearview.

You turn around in your seat, and watch the antler bob up and down, banging and falling against the hood of the cab.

"A zombie," he says. "Sucker's not dead."

"Let me do it," you say.

Behind the truck, you are afraid to open the hatch. You get a rock from the side of the road, and it, too, is heavier than you thought it would be.

Pushing the buck down, you give all your body weight, rock in hand. And when it gets up, you slam it down again. Suddenly, your father wrestles Darryl, a fight between a man and something else. The buck has no wings to flap, no guttural calls until you rock him in the head, his hair glinting a color so all you can think is Mrs. Mills. Her nylon legs. Your mother's nasal voice. A bound cashier. Each crack releases all that energy. With every hit, you let out a call from your stomach. You and the buck grunting in anger. Dumb corpse. Thud again. Your hand looks stronger and older against the rock until you can't tell where it stops, and your fingers begin. You keep going long after the buck stopped moving because the gut sounds set the beat of your pace.

"Hey," the driver calls. "I think you got him. Pretty sure he's good and dead now." He'd back away, running, if he weren't driving the truck.

You slam the rock hard into the buck's eye until it falls into its skull. Before you know, the truck revs and pulls the rock away from you. Staring at your hands, you recognize their work, the blood pulsing beneath your skin, and from somewhere in the trees, you hear night sounds.

When you walk up, covered in blood, Mrs. Mills is on the porch.

"James," she says. "What on earth?"

Her hair is down past her shoulders, and, to you, she seems older, now, more matronly.

"Just an accident. A deer," you say.

She brings you to the kitchen, hands you a glass of lemonade as though you've had a hard day of work.

You sit at the table, and when you set the glass down, notice it has a smudge of maroon on it—fingerprints.

She suggests calling your mother. You aren't sure.

The faucet runs, and she hands you a washcloth to wipe off the blood.

What We Do Here on Earth

Though Winnie should be wearing black to her ex-husband's funeral, she's not.

She enters the viewing room, cluttered with people she hasn't seen since she and Lawrence were married, and who've probably forgotten her name, perhaps misplace the fact that she had, at one time, been Lawrence's shiny new bride.

Winnie sees her: Lucy. She lingers alone, between the bowl of pillow-mints and the coat rack. Her flowy skirt and peasant shirt make her look like a ghost. She isn't wearing black either, but a lavender color. The two of them—Winnie and Lucy—dressed like Lawrence hasn't just died, among all the stiff black and charcoal and dark brown.

Winnie wonders if Lucy, or if any of these unknown women, or even those listed by name in the obituary, knew the Lawrence who insisted their house was haunted, who, at some point in the recent past, stopped attending Our Lady of Mercy masses in exchange for what he called Mystic Circles at Lake Ontario? The Lawrence who spent hours what looked like staring at the moon in their back yard? Do they know he smoked cannabis in the basement? Do they know, regardless of the sensitive schmuck Winnie accused him of being, he never cried—not even when she miscarried once, or even after the third loss, when the doctor told her it "Wasn't in the cards?" Not even when he told Winnie he'd "been" with Lucy the night Winnie locked her keys in the car while it was running and she needed him? And even when he left her, his overnight bag on his shoulder as though he'd be right back—even when she was crying and Nixon was whimpering—still, not then, not to make them feel better about themselves, did he cry. When the blue stone fell from his hand as he left, he stopped, picked it up, and walked out.

There were so many who filled Lawrence's life after the divorce. Winnie knows those people are here, those closer to Lawrence. Lucy is one of them.

The room fills Winnie with memories of her mother, whose funeral she held in this room just last spring. Teddy, Lawrence's brother, is the most visibly sad at the funeral competition. He stands next to the casket and shakes the hands of people Winnie recognizes but can't name, especially not in their funeral uniforms.

Winnie keeps an eye on Lucy, who stands with her hands clasped in front of her, a tissue wadded between her fingers that she tastefully dabs to her eyes and nose from time to time.

When Winnie approaches Teddy, she tries not to look down by her knee, where Lawrence's dead, clay-like face sits at the head of the coffin. Teddy clamps his arms around Winnie, pulling her into his firm belly, then pulls away, shaking his bobbly head and grabbing her hand too tight.

"Teddy. Hi," is all Winnie says.

"He was just alive," Teddy says, "five days ago. Manning our garage sale." He lets out a sort of gurgle. He keeps her hand in his as though he's not ready to see the person behind her in the sympathy line. "Just stay here a minute," Teddy says. "Look at him. When was the last time you saw him, Winnie?"

Winnie can't look. She focuses on Teddy's face, the red blotches around his cheeks and the sheen at his nostrils.

"I was wondering about Nixon. The least I can do is take him off your hands," Winnie says about the black shepherd she and Lawrence took in just before they married. Winnie tries to remember why Lawrence had custody of Nixon in the first place. The dog was meant as unofficial practice for children, and they both appreciated naming the dog Nixon for different reasons. Winnie, as a form of reverence, and Lawrence, because he'd liked the thought of walking Nixon on a leash and scolding him when he pooped on the floor.

"You should ask Lucy. I let her take him," Teddy says.

"Well, now is a good time to have him come back home to live," Winnie says. Then she thinks again about what he's just said: *Lucy*, her stomach clenching. "He is my dog," Winnie says. "He's licensed in Lawrence's and my name." The one thing Winnie could have any claim to —imagine if they had children. Imagine.

"I know, and Lucy came for Nixon right after Lawrence died. If you wanted him—"

"It's been four days. Christ," Winnie says, her mother's scolding for using the name in vain flashing through her mind. Winnie gives Teddy a kiss on the cheek, a squeeze of the hand, and walks away. It has been four days. Four days during which her couch was her perch, and outside the window, the Neighborhood Watch posted flyers in response to a recent spate of burglaries Nixon should be the perfect guard against. It would have been a blessing could Winnie muster enough space in her mind for simple fears.

After Lawrence moved out, he brought Nixon around to visit every other day. He dropped him off for a few hours and went off wherever he went that Winnie refused to give him the satisfaction of asking about—sometimes, she imagined it was a benign outing like down to this Taproom or that Saloon for cards with friends, and sometimes, she suspected, it was something more threatening (threatening to what? Their dissolved marriage?) like a blind date with someone he didn't realize he already knew and hated, or a completely willing date with someone—like Lucy, who will now be walking Nixon around Winnie's block.

For Winnie, in divorce, sadness came with the loss in objects—one pillow on the king bed, a single cup of tea, which Winnie never drinks, on the buffet, Lawrence's apple butter extradited from the fridge. But Nixon. The house echoed after he left, but his absence became palpable, almost more present than his actual body was before the divorce.

When Lawrence stopped bringing the dog, Winnie became frantic to know why. Nixon's visit was an essential part of her routine. When she drank her coffee after work, she expected him at her feet, wanting to play tug-of-war with one of Lawrence's knee socks he'd left behind, knotted in the middle.

Teddy carries on through the service, his body quaking with every sob, his stature making him the more likely of the two brothers to die of a heart attack.

After the indoor service ends, Lucy's scraggly flower-child hair drifts in the wind as they walk to the plot, and Winnie can't stop watching her from behind, how even when she walks in a straight line, she seems like she's wandering.

Lucy ends up near Teddy, and her position as next of kin hits Winnie like a gut punch.

Winnie sidles up next to Lucy and pretends she doesn't notice it's her.

"Lucy," Teddy says, and Winnie waits to hear what comes next, but nothing. She wishes she were standing between them. Lawrence has become more precious now that he's untouchable, now that being with him isn't an option for any of them.

Lucy looks directly at Winnie. "Winnie," she says, tucking hair behind her ears.

"Yeah," Winnie says. Lucy hugs her. "I'm sorry," she says. "I'm so sorry."

Teddy leans over to Lucy.

"Leave her alone, Lucy," Teddy says. His lips and eyes are swollen. "Just because he's dead doesn't change what you did."

Lucy apologizes again and stares at the coffin where the man the two women loved lies. Winnie doesn't know what Lucy and Lawrence shared —she didn't let Lawrence go into details beyond the séance where they'd met. Lawrence and Winnie never considered they might stay together. They immediately began mourning something they couldn't get back.

Lucy looks at Winnie again, and Winnie wishes she would just stop. It isn't that she's annoying, it's worse. It's maybe Lucy could have given Lawrence a child or maybe, now, Lucy will insist on keeping Nixon. What if Lucy is pregnant?

"My mother is buried over there," Lucy says.

"Yeah," Winnie says.

"Your mother died, too, didn't she? Last year?" Lucy asks, and it scares Winnie that Lucy's so invested, and then she says, "She wants me to tell you she's okay." Lucy gazes at Winnie as though she's forgiving her for something.

"What?" Winnie says.

"She's okay, she tells me. She wants you to know. And Larry, too, says he's just fine."

"Lawrence, you mean?"

"Sorry. I called him Larry," Lucy says, suddenly avoiding Winnie's eyes.

"The dead can't tell me anything. And you can't tell me anything about Lawrence I don't already know."

Teddy bites his lip and shakes his head, covers his ears with his hands because perhaps this is obscene. It's as if Winnie watches all of this unfold from another world. No one around hears the exchange, which makes it feel even less likely to be happening.

"You're full of shit," Teddy says, pointing, nearly putting his finger to Lucy's nose. "Just go."

But Winnie leaves instead and realizes later she's missed her opportunity to ask Lucy for Nixon. And probably no one besides Teddy and Lucy knows why it's so awful she's leaving when she does, that Lawrence once called Winnie the love of his life, it all meant something, once.

At home after the funeral, when she's alone, Winnie decides to let herself cry for five minutes, set by the kitchen timer, which she's brought into the front room—the first living room. When they bought their house, they'd needed two living spaces. They needed this 1855 Victorian with 2600 square feet. And since, it seems to have grown, first, doubling in size when Winnie realized they'd never have children, and by the time Lawrence moved out, it tripled in size, but he took Nixon, too, so it added another half-a-floor's worth of space from nowhere, and now Lawrence has died, it's a yawning field. Winnie can hardly feel the walls, though she knows there are pictures hanging on them.

Winnie watches her neighbor Fannie walk slowly across Erie Ave, but with purpose, to her porch. Fannie, the first to treat Winnie as if Lawrence's death was her loss, too. And she was the only one to phone Winnie when the burglaries began and phones almost daily with updates —the latest, two nights ago, when the burglars broke into the Brodskys' home while they were at a bridge night. Winnie can't blame Fannie for wanting to stir up excitement in her life (that has, in this last stage, amounted to her 12-hour patrol of Erie Avenue from her front windows).

Fannie is small and solid with orthopedic shoes and red lipstick, the closest living thing to Winnie. At any moment, Winnie could see Fannie from the window of her front parlor.

47

The timer sounds, scaring Winnie. She'd forget the private time for tears.

The doorbell trills.

"Banana bread," Fannie says from the other side of the door. She pants lightly and wears a tomato-splotched potholder on each hand. "Still hot," she says and heads past Winnie to the kitchen, where she sets the pan on the oven.

"Thanks, but—"

"Listen. Why are you staying here alone? And do you know Lucy Baxter has walked Nixon by my house every morning and afternoon since Lawrence died?" Fannie hates Nixon. She's so afraid of dogs she won't cross the street if she sees him on the porch. "You need that dog. That thing will protect you."

"She walks him past your house?" Winnie asks. She wonders, *Does Nixon ever pull toward home? Does Lucy struggle to keep Winnie's dog on her side of the street?*

"Right after the morning edition arrives and then again before the streetlights come on. I don't know why she's walking so close to dark. I'm sure she's seen the fliers." Fannie gestures toward the bread. "A grief gift. I need the pan back."

Winnie almost invites Fannie for dinner, but the old woman gives a stiff wave of her hand before walking to the door.

When the phone rings, it's Teddy, and he half-guffaws/half-sobs, says, "I'm calling from the other side to tell you I'm sorry I gave Nixon to Lucy."

"Man, what a lunatic, that Lucy," Winnie says. "I want Nixon back."

"Come have a drink with us, Winnie. We're at Barber's. You know, if you get too worried—shit, with the robberies and all—you could always come stay until they catch them, or at least for the night."

"Thanks, but I'm not up for it, Teddy," Winnie says.

"You know Lawrence, though. He believed all that shit, too. Maybe that's why... he and Lucy... you know..." Teddy says. Winnie wishes the phone would cut out.

"That's why *what*? You think he fell for her because she believes in ghosts?"

"That was dumb of me to say. Forget it."

But even after they hang up, she can't.

The night Winnie's father died, Lawrence had called to ask about his death. He told Winnie her father wanted to tell her he loved her very much. How could one small village have two mediums? Now, Winnie wonders if Lawrence passed along that message from Lucy.

The moment Winnie's father died, it was as simple as being on the phone and then hanging up.

And then Lawrence made it seem as though the dead could call back.

She tries to imagine where life goes, the life her father sent out in his last breath, all the love Lawrence did or didn't have in the last moments of his life. She knew Heaven was the answer her mother would give her.

Winnie's mother died in a fitful way, the nurses said. She cried out for her father, and then her breathing grew quiet, and Lawrence was the one to tell Winnie she'd died. He called her from his home in the middle of the night and said it outright: "Call the nursing home. Your mother died. I feel it," Lawrence said.

Winnie hung up on him. And then the phone rang. It was the nursing home.

Minutes later, Winnie called Lawrence back and asked him to stay overnight with her. She wasn't sure why he agreed to come. When he apologized, and Winnie asked what for, he said, "Because your mother died."

By then, he was sitting on the couch in the front parlor. And he said, "There are people who can sense these things. There are people who are open to knowing what else there is besides what we do here on earth. Look, I'm sorry I called to tell you about your mother dying."

"Lucky guess," Winnie said.

Lawrence shrugged. "You just need to be more open," he said.

They slept together that night. It was the only time after their divorce and awkward as the first time, like they'd grown into different people even though they were the same couple that agreed to use birth control just to stop the losses.

It wasn't until later, and still, Winnie imagines Lawrence and Lucy probably had spiritual, transcendent sex all the time.

Of course, Winnie watches out the window for Lucy to walk Nixon past her house. She set her alarm for early in the morning, but apparently not early enough—the morning edition was already at her doorstep. She'd napped all day and drank tea, and now she finishes the banana bread with some whiskey as she sits by the window at dusk. She can see Fannie's silhouette in the living room light.

Winnie watches, still, as Fannie stands and opens her door. The wind pushes leaves around in the street and a newspaper catches on a tree trunk. As Lucy approaches Fannie's house, Fannie steps out of her porch onto the first step and trips to the sidewalk, landing in an embarrassing position. Lucy rushes to her side, and Nixon bounds over, licking Fannie's terrified face.

With Lucy's help, Fannie stands. Winnie wishes she could hear their conversation. Lucy nods her head and shakes her head and nods her head again and pulls the hair from her face. Fannie points at Nixon and then to Winnie's porch. And then again, at Winnie's porch, and then, at Winnie's porch, again. Fannie's eyebrows are nearly at her hairline. She grabs Nixon's leash, and Lucy steps away with her hands raised as if an innocent.

When Lucy turns the corner, Fannie lets Nixon lead her across the street to Winnie's house.

That night, Winnie makes Spanish rice, her mother's version. She'd tried again to get Fannie to stay.

"I'm not coming into this house again now that Nixon's back," Fannie said, dropping Nixon's leash. Winnie wonders what Fannie's eating for dinner.

She doesn't bother with the math for just one portion. And she smiles as she thinks of her mother, who would cook "enough for a goddamn army," her father always said. Winnie's refrigerator is full of leftovers. Throwing them out has become a ritual.

She drops a square of pepper to Nixon, who turns up his nose. A few times in the front living room today, Nixon perked up his ears to another frequency. He barks at the empty doorway of the kitchen, and Winnie thinks of Lucy and her spirits, shaking her head, half-angry because Lucy surrendered Nixon so easily, like she was some sort of saint. Winnie pushes from her mind the thought she should be grateful to Lucy. Instead, she'll bring Fannie a bowl of Spanish rice.

Nixon's snout rests on the crest of her foot, secures her with the weight of his head. The more she thinks about it, Winnie begins to feel like death is a party thrown without her.

At the party, Winnie imagines her mother is smoking a cigarette with Lawrence, and her father "rests his eyes" in front of the newspaper. Her mother leans toward Lawrence to say, "She never uses enough chili powder in that rice. Or garlic."

Lawrence nods even though he never liked it. "Or salt," he says.

Winnie adds more of all three to the pot.

When Winnie looks down at her feet, there is Nixon, and he is what she has.

Tonight, the dog sleeps soundly at the side of Winnie's bed, though only after spending about an hour staring at the alarm clock, which made static noises though she turned it off. Winnie wakes, startled by a banging sound, and listens for wind, but a glance out the window reveals still branches. There's more banging, and the radio fizzles, and Winnie's somehow relieved and maybe thankful to see what's happening here. *Turn on the light*, she challenges Lawrence from her mind.

"Lawrence?" she calls out to him. Her sleepy mind shifts to her mother, in her last breaths, calling out for her father.

Nixon barks.

A flicker of light spills beneath her bedroom door, and she can make out two males arguing. "Go! Go!" they say. And all Winnie's family— Lawrence, her mother and her cries for her father, are gone again. The burglars are in her home. Winnie was next, is all.

Footsteps pound down the front stairs, and Winnie says any prayer she can think of under her breath, which amounts to *Please, God*. She follows Nixon to the bedroom door, where he barks incessantly. When she imagines it's safe, she opens the door to the hall, and the dog bounds down the stairs and out the wide-open front door. Winnie stands on the threshold. Fannie's porch light glows and Nixon's shadow casts large on the lawn, a snout pointing, perhaps, at things Winnie can't see.

Where To?

The girl never thought she'd pick up a hitchhiker. Her only experience with hitchhikers was on road trips, passing a few haggard, sloppy men with tired eyes and thumbs in the air. They were archetypes in flannel, ripped jeans, or a dirty white t-shirt. Hitchhikers were both dangerous and vulnerable. Maybe they came from another time. She felt relieved, though a little sad, when they were out of sight.

"Hey uhh, listen," was the first thing Rich said to her, tapping her on the shoulder in the gas station on Route 104. She tensed. She didn't like going into gas stations to begin with. Usually, she opted for the full-service stations, where she didn't have to leave the car, where she could avoid any possible interaction with the carnie-types who ran the registers or the robbers seen on *Cops*, their guns and masks threatening the camera above them. But it was completely light out at eleven-thirty in the morning.

Maybe she thought giving a ride to a stranger was better than being held up. Maybe the girl thought this was the equivalent of being held up.

"I need a ride home," he continued. His face was covered with little blond fuzz. He seemed younger than her and maybe that made him less intimidating. Maybe it was his light hair.

"It's cold. Could ya just give me a ride?"

The girl didn't like the impatience in his voice. She glanced up and down. No visible weapons. She didn't know where this was going.

After he finished his sentence, she remembered to breathe. Would she ever be home again? She imagined her cat, sitting on her ratty yellow sofa, purring and licking her fur.

What did it look like in her house right then? How was the light coming through the window? She felt the sort of frustration she'd felt when she'd locked her keys in the car a few days earlier and had thought, while looking through the window, Why can't I just be on the other side of this pane? The girl wanted to be in her car on her way home, in a way she usually hated to be: alone. She would call her mother while she did the dishes, her sister while she was chopping veggies for dinner. She lived alone and her imagination ran wild with stories from the books she read to not feel so alone. The girl wanted to be alone though, now, in her car.

She knew she was shaking, because he put his hand on her wrist to stop her car keys from jingling. Bold, the girl thought. His hand was cold and rough. She ripped her arm away.

"Where to?" she asked. She couldn't believe it.

"Just on the Ridge," he said, scratching behind his ear. She was still eyeing him, trying to place him in society. Where did he work? A garage, maybe. Was he a grocery clerk? No. How do you know, the girl thought. Maybe he was a receptionist. The owner of a soup-kitchen. Maybe she could ask him what he did for a living.

"My car broke down a mile or so back, and I haven't been able to get a ride," he said.

She thought of *Lifetime* movies. No, the girl would be thinking if she were home watching this scene in frames, you're so stupid. Do not let him in your car. She created the scene in her mind: the jingle of a bell on the door of the gas station, breaking silence, the girl leaving with the hitchhiker and never reappearing in the movie except on posters with the word MISSING. It would be a close-up picture with a smiling face in black and white, specs below.

The girl imagined what picture her family would use for her.

She didn't really remember how they ended up in the car. It was hot though, because the heat was on high, and she was nervous. It was a cold day, and the western New York weather made the girl realize why this man was so desperate for a ride. The mudded snow was climbing to giant mounds that lined parking lots of endless strip malls and car dealerships. Ridge Road was the only road the girl was familiar with, really, because she'd just moved from Ithaca and hadn't gone far beyond.

She'd moved to Bridgeport for work. "It's a temporary situation," the voice from the corporate office told her. She'd told herself this, too. She was a buyer for "the corporate devil," as her brother-in-law said to her. She was, and she'd liked it for a while. Now she spent afternoons sitting in a cold store on SUNY Bridgeport's campus, deciding what the best market was for trade books in the area: Oprah's book club? Chick-lit? She designed themes of the month. This month, January, was Women's Month. If the girl listened to her mother, the selection would be narrowed to cookbooks and interior design. Her mother, "a woman of tradition," according to herself. "Turn it back around," she'd told the girl. "Feminism is dead. Make a difference," her mother said. "Take your husband's name—if you ever get married," she'd said to the girl. In response, the girl ordered books by Bell Hooks, Betty Friedan, and Sylvia Plath. None of which she'd read.

He told the girl his name was Rich. He didn't mention a job. His car was old, he said, an Escort. He asked where she was living. While she was dumb enough to pick him up, she wasn't about to tell him which complex she lived in.

The girl thought back to her place. Yesterday, at exactly this moment, what was she doing? At this moment yesterday, she had no idea she would be in this sort of danger exactly twenty-four hours from then. She'd been sitting in her kitchen, staring at the dripping faucet she would now welcome, talking to her mother on the phone. Her mother sounded farther away then. The girl knew it was all in her head.

The radio in the car was on the college station, and she thought of asking him his taste in music. The girl imagined most kidnappers listen to classic rock. If she was nice, she thought, maybe he wouldn't hurt her. Instead, he reached his hand over and adjusted the tuner himself. He really won't be in the car that long, the girl thought. Is changing the station necessary? He left it on soft rock. The Bryan Adams song she'd heard too many times. It made her queasy.

Here she was, driving down a long road with no sidewalks. Cars passed so quickly they surely could not see her here with this man she didn't know, driving to places she didn't know how to get to. In Ithaca, the girl would probably know this man. In Ithaca, she could reach out her window to the people on the sidewalk, chatting and eating at cafes, riding bikes, gardening. They'd be watching. She could tap someone on the shoulder. *Help me*, she'd say.

Her mother's voice was shaking yesterday at noon as they were on the phone and her mother told the girl this: "I lost a tooth. Can you believe it?" Her mother, at the age of fifty-seven, lost her first adult tooth. The girl desperately searched her unfamiliar apartment for something concrete of her mother. She'd stolen these cheap souvenir spoons from her before she'd left. They hung on her kitchen wall in a wooden holder. Most had state names engraved on them: Hawaii, Rhode Island, New York, Colorado—places her mother ran off to at different times of her life for boyfriends, husband, family. The girl looked at the collection and imagined her mother poking at her soft gums in the mirror, her black mascara leaking a little at the corners of her eyes. *How ugly I look*, her mother would have been thinking. And really, the girl understood her mother's concern, staring at her mother's spoon collection, because since the last time she talked to her mother, there was less of her living, breathing body on this planet. Her mother's body would continue in this pattern, the girl thought, until there was none left on this earth. A little piece of her nicotine-stained enamel in the garbage. The girl knew this because she'd asked. "Do you have it still? Can you send it to me?" "No, honey," her mother said. "Why would I keep it?" She'd pictured the surprised look her mother's face.

The land here was cold and boring and hard. Ithaca had movement, hills. Ithaca had her mother. The girl argued with her sister, who'd left long ago with her family, that she would be sorry when their mother died. "What will you think?" the girl asked. "You'll look back at all that missed time if something happens." She'd insisted her sister would wake up and feel in her stomach someone from home was no longer living. "I couldn't fathom the guilt," the girl said.

Most people the girl had shared this opinion with, including her sister, laughed at her. Her mother had scolded her. "I hate it when you're morbid," her mother would say with a cigarette between her fingers and a wooden spoon in her other hand, stirring a large pot of sauce, the tomato jumped and spattered the sides, her shirt, the stove. Of course, her mother would always tack on: "Although you never know what can happen. Things can happen to us here, at home, too, if you leave."

Now, the girl thought to herself, her insides so tense they hurt, this is your payment for leaving her.

"Got any kids?" he asked the girl.

"No," the girl said. *Kids, ha.*

"You know, I won't be around forever," her mother had said to her. This revelation could be in reference to a million things: a bad fight when the girl was a teenager, and she'd scream "I hate you!" or when she refused to go grocery shopping with her mother because she had better things to do. Only, when her mother was talking about children, it was usually followed with a comment like, "Jesum! I'll be long gone by the time you have Charlie!" Her mother had picked out names, but was *only kidding.*

"What about you?" The girl's hands were stiff to the wheel at ten and two.

"Yeah… two boys. Two and… four or five," he said. She relaxed a little. She took a minute to look at him closer. He didn't fit her profile of a hitchhiker, really. He wore a simple long-sleeved t-shirt with an orange puffy vest and a pair of blue sweatpants. The girl imagined his children at home, little miniatures of himself, running around amid dirty dishes, a television blaring in the background, toy guns aimed at each other. "Bang," they would yell.

"Oh. Nice," she said. A couple seconds passed, or minutes. "Names?" she'd stopped talking in complete sentences.

"Yeah, Adam and Ben," Rich said. "My girlfriend picked them out." He seemed to sadden. The girl was afraid he was going to lay it on thick: a sappy story about how his girlfriend left with the children. Suddenly, the girl pictured an empty apartment with next to nothing—a box of stale doughnuts, a half-eaten sandwich on the counter, a stained mattress with no sheets on the floor. But he was silent.

She drove on for a few miles with few instructions. She began to think she might make it home.

"Hey, can you make a right here?" He tapped his fingers on the passenger's window, making little circles in the condensation on the glass. Fingerprints, the girl thought. "I thought your house was on Ridge," she said. She'd taken to calling it "Ridge" the way everyone did here, as though it were a destination. It was simply a road that followed a geological ridge, stretching for miles and peppered with crosses where people had crashed and died in the wicked winters.

"Yeah, but I remembered a buddy of mine lives here and I need to pay him some money," he said.

"So, you want me to drop you off here instead?" the girl asked.

"No. Don't leave. Wait here. I'll be right back," he said.

Yeah right, she thought. She planned to back out of the driveway the minute he closed the door behind him, squealing and grinding if she had to.

"Seriously," he said. "You're not gonna go anywhere, are ya?"

He slammed the door shut.

He left the car and walked to the house, a sort of slumpy walk. Surely, she should not have let someone who walked like *that* into her car. Although she'd been driving with him, she sat and tried to remember what he looked like in the face: his eyes, near or far apart? His nose, pointed, bulbous, hooked? Was his chin pronounced? Would she have enough for a composite sketch?

She should have been driving away. She had plenty of time. Nine minutes, actually, by the time Rich would return. The girl should have sped away, but she thought of herself, sitting in her apartment with the radio on at all times, staring through the windows, watching the few people who were in the complex wander to their cars with grocery bags or baby seats, shutting their doors behind them. And Rich, wandering around the side roads, trying to find a ride to get to his kids. It was enough for her to sit. To wait. He scrambled from the house as though he expected her car to be gone, a small trail of smoke behind her. He smiled when he saw the car. She realized then he was smiling for the relief of warmth, a ride. He wasn't having the same panicked reaction to what was happening. He was not grateful to be breathing as she was. He wasn't imagining the last moments of his life, as the girl did when his weight hit the passenger's side of her car.

She shouldn't have been surprised when the door opened and cold slapped her in the face. He cleared his throat as he got in, smelling of cigarette smoke.

"Yeah, alright," he said. "Thanks. Just one more stop though, okay?"

"Fine, fine," she said, although she was annoyed. If he is going to steal me, I would rather him just do it and get it over with, she thought.

The girl never asked where they were going. She just let him tell her where to drive.

The sun wasn't shining, but the girl could see the specks of dust floating in the air above the dash. They swirled and made her nauseous. How driving slowly through parking lots, searching for spaces, made her nauseous, the way this day, in its slowly ticking minutes and dragging stops, made her nauseous.

"Damn, I really could use a cup of coffee," he said. "Want one?"

Over the past few weeks, the girl took to eating chocolate covered espresso beans as a replacement for her mother's coffee. She didn't even want to start drinking it in the first place, really. "Come on," the girl's mother said. "You can't be Italian and not drink coffee." Sure, she could. But eventually she gave into this notion of being like her mother. Along with vials of anti-aging creams and a dozen-or-so pairs of sunglasses to keep her from squinting, the girl also decided to take up drinking coffee at twenty-four. At first, she'd swirl in vanilla creamers or chocolate-covered spoons so she could enjoy it. Slowly, she'd decided to use a couple sugars and regular creamer: *Cremora*, her mother called it regardless of the brand. Eventually, the girl drank black coffee and felt sophisticated. Now, she'd realized she couldn't imitate her mother's coffee and chomped on espresso beans.

When Rich came out of the fourth gas station they'd passed that morning, he held two cups of coffee in his hands. She stared at his sweatpants. It seemed like déjà vu every time she'd watch his legs approach the car, a stain on the right thigh and a hole down toward the ankle. This, too, was in slow motion to her. The girl knew his feet were making noise and the way she couldn't hear it from the other side of the window bothered her. Then, she saw his arm from the same angle, grabbing at the handle and eventually, she watched his ear as he fastened his seatbelt. What hitchhiker does that?

"Here, I gotcha one." His face was proud, smirking as he held the Styrofoam cup to the girl. The hair around his face was overgrown and wisped around into little curls and then he seemed younger again.

"Thanks," the girl said. "Now where do I drop you off?" The girl's mother would have killed her if she knew how she'd spent this morning.

"No, I said one more stop," he said.

"That was it. That *was* the 'one more stop,'" the girl said.

"No," he said. "Then we wanted coffee," he said.

"We?" The girl raised her eyebrows.

"Whatever, fine... *I* did," he said. "So can you just stop at the hardware store, then you can bring me to my place?"

The hardware store? she thought.

"You're not picking up anything gigantic, are you? It's not like my car's huge or anything," she said.

"No, no. I just need a small square of indoor/outdoor carpeting," he said.

To wrap my body in before he lets it fall into Lake Ontario, the girl thought.

"Huh?" she asked.

"I have to carpet my niece's playhouse," he said.

"Your niece? You building one for your kids, too?"

"Actually, I don't have kids," he said, and let out a little laugh.

"What? But you—"

"Yeah, I thought maybe if I said I had kids, I'd seem less scary," he said. "You know, you'd give me a ride and well, then I could get some errands done today."

"You lied, then. Nice," the girl said. She'd imagined children that never even existed. "So where'd you get the names then? I mean, I don't even remember what they were, but how'd you pull those out of the air?"

"They're the same ones I always use," he said, lighting up a cigarette.

"Oh, you aren't going to ask if you can smoke that?"

"Can I smoke this?"

"Yeah, fine," the girl said. "My mother smokes."

"Oh," he said.

The girl thought maybe he would have asked about her mother. How old? What does she do? Where is she?

"Yeah she does, she smokes. Her name is Gladys—it actually is, I don't just tell people that," the girl said. A few seconds passed, and he didn't respond. "Hey, what do you mean the same names you always use? You do this often?"

"Eh, only when it's cold, and I have a lot of stuff to take care of," he said. "I've become a pro at small talk."

The girl supposed the whole car deal was a lie, too.

She pulled into the slushy gravel parking lot of Stall's Hardware.

"Here," she said.

"Hey, thanks," he said. "Gimme a few."

He really didn't want to know more about my mother, the girl thought. The girl would call her mother when she got home and tell her about this, and she would shake her head at the girl from the other line between sips of cold coffee.

He was in Stall's for about ten minutes. There was a wooden bench outside painted a dull green, to match the store. She considered getting out to stretch, then thought maybe Rich would see her and think she was in no hurry to get home. And she was. She had been the whole time.

There were piles of broken brick and stone piled outside the entrance, dripping with water from snow melting in the gutter. *Pavers*, the girl's father called those heavy stones while building a patio behind their house. The girl's mother sat and watched him every day last summer. The girl's father dragged each into its place as her mother watched, smiling occasionally, picking at her nails, rough at the edges from gardening or washing dishes. Her mother got up only to empty the ash tray or grab her father fresh ice water.

Rich approached the car again, a small roll of green carpeting tucked under his arm. He opened the door in the same way he'd done the other times that day and stooped down.

"You know what? I think I'm just gonna walk back to my place," he said plainly.

"What? You gonna carry that?"

"Yeah, it's good. I'll walk. No sweat," he said.

The girl looked over at the shadow he left against the side of the building.

"Okay, well," she said.

He said nothing but shut the door. The girl sat in the parking lot a minute, watching him stroll away with the carpeting under his left arm until she could only see his silhouette.

Dear Victor, If I Could Write You a Letter

The evening before your departure for Berlin, when we hugged goodbye, I need you to know I wasn't trying to kiss you. Though we grew close over the winter during our shifts at Quaker Maid, you <u>are</u> married, as you say, and <u>not my kind</u> if you aren't. Besides, there was Clara, just down the street, manning the fort, feeding your children, setting her hair to see you off. I was your ear outside family life. And it isn't as though I haven't been rejected before, and though <u>you didn't need to reject me</u>, you <u>did</u>, and it's been caught in my mind ever since.

Twenty-five, rail-thin, and wearing a simple Quaker Maid uniform—a starched blue shift with the white hat, I felt childish and awkward when I ran into Clara on the sidewalk weeks ago. In a panic, I initially wondered if you mentioned to Clara how <u>you</u> <u>suspected</u> I tried to kiss you, though by this writing, I know you did.

Clara approached me as though to spread gospel. She can't get "a wink of sleep" and the babies cry for you all the time. And Quaker Maid. "It's too much," she said. (Oh! I asked Clara to help with the annual Quaker Maid tomato harvest—we <u>need</u> the extra help to can the harvest before it spoils.)

I told Clara your family life would get better for lack of anything else to say. All I know are her angry scolds from across the street at suppertime (and the cries from the children). It's hard to imagine Clara's life, so full—"too much," even—that she can't bear it when I have fantasies of children and arranging furniture in a house I don't own.

Clara brought her face close to mine, and asked, "Have you ever felt like your only love has left for good?"

<u>Of course not</u>.

Then—and this is how it all started—she told me about the clanging noise she'd heard some time around midnight, maybe trash cans rustling around or maybe the sounds of a man taller than anyone in this neighborhood. With just us, now, in the neighborhood, we're on high alert at the reports of the Church Street Prowler.

And so, when Clara grew upset about you, I listened. She asked me to come with her and Betty to find the prowler. She hadn't laid out any real plan. Had we wanted to find the prowler? Then what? She told me she was sure she was losing her mind, here, alone. The children, she says, are so much.

Clara said we'd show him we weren't scared. "He'll run," she said. "I have a bat—two of them. We'll bring them," she said, patting at her curlers with her fingertips. She said her scalp itched. Her whole body "was in revolt."

It was the least I could do. I didn't have anything else to do.

The Quaker Maid lot is full of tomatoes, overripe with red bubbles to be canned and eaten by you hungry soldiers on the other side of a wide ocean. At the end of my shift, I stop at the outskirts of the lot to see if the workers have made a dent in the stockpile. It always seems to have grown, somehow, instead of shrunken, as though we're all working backwards. So much that on Friday, I think it might do better to rewind to Monday, with its much smaller pile of juice and seeds.

I've come to know so much about Mrs. Leiter, she seems more than my landlady. Because of her overboard vigilance, I assumed she would have mentioned any bumps in the dark she'd heard, but she asked me, instead, when I expected to be home from Quaker Maid and if I would have dinner with her.

That evening, she made spaghetti. With the surplus of tomatoes, all anyone makes anymore is spaghetti. At dinner, I began to feel as though I'd missed my whole life and sat with a friend on our deathbeds. There's not much <u>life</u> to my life.

I asked Mrs. Leiter if she heard anything about the prowler.

I could imagine Clara's fear—and my version of Clara's fear is only imagined—who should I feel protective of? Mrs. Leiter? I'm the only tenant in a house painted mauve that smells like eucalyptus or a funeral home. She <u>has</u> lived a whole life.

Mrs. Leiter said she'd read in the paper, but wouldn't be surprised if everyone was just hearing ghosts. "And did you know Mr. Leiter died of a heart attack on the front porch?" She always calls her dead husband Mr. Leiter. When he was living, she probably called him an endearment like *Sugar* or *Darling*.

"Shooting stars tonight," Mrs. Leiter told me out of nowhere.

Supposedly, we're crossing with meteors at the time I'm writing this and will have long crossed by the time you get to read this. Which is never.

With all the men away, the women here are untethered and vigilant. I suspect Mrs. Leiter and I share a sense of finally belonging, as neither of us had anyone to lean on before the war, and now we're just two of many, compelled to lean on each another.

That night, at dinner, Mrs. Leiter asked me if I'd care for the house after she dies. I asked if she was ill, and she said she's just old. I tried to imagine myself in a future, and I couldn't. I certainly couldn't be Clara.

What should I have said? Would this solidify my place? Will I die in this same house in much the same manner as Mrs. Leiter does? She promised she'll haunt me! Said she knows the pain of asking for a sign from Mr. Leiter and receiving nothing. Said she'll leave hydrangeas on the table.

When I hesitated, Mrs. Leiter told me she saw the two of us, me and you, walking home from a shift at the Quaker Maid. She'd been out on her porch watching for a neighbor, who, she insists, secretly plants weeds in her garden. Instead, she saw me with you. She called you "Clara's husband" and raised her eyebrows. She'd been married nine years by my age, she noted. I was running out of options, she said.

I don't remember making any choices. It's easy to feel on the outside of the world.

I worried that conversation was some sort of contract, and when Mrs. Leiter asked me again if I'd accept the house, I said, "Sure," mostly out of confusion. I cleared my throat half a dozen times and took bite after bite of spaghetti and hungrily drank the whole glass of water before excusing myself. I scrambled up the back winding staircase to my room with sloped ceilings, where I could breathe.

I'd caught wind of my future. When I looked out the window, I swore I saw a neighbor cutting the asters from Mrs. Leiter's garden. Looking again, no one was there.

Your house was lit up like a celebration if I didn't know any better. The kitchen was warm and smelled of pasta water and tomato sauce. Of course, I was the first to doubt Clara, but sure enough, I heard a tap on your kitchen window, and of course, Clara tugged at my sleeve to pay attention. And then, like a child, she pinched me, hard, on the arm, angry enough to go outside, hunting the prowler. I never would have imagined Clara had the guts, even with her assertive personality. She wiped her hands on her apron. She looked tired. Worried. Her hair gone frizzy in the steamy kitchen, and the corners of her mouth pulled down. I had an instinct to hug her, but I didn't. She stared out the window and sighed, wishing, I imagine, to be somewhere else.

Your children were at the end of a row of cabinets, standing one behind another behind the other, grumbling or whimpering or crying. The children were missing something, and they all looked for it in different directions. Then their glances fell on me. I don't think I've spoken to a child since I was one myself. When I bent to say hello, they flinched.

I didn't know what to say, so I asked their names. I knew I would recognize them from our conversations but couldn't have come up with them on my own at the time. Your oldest, Benjamin, resembles you so much I can imagine he bears the brunt of Clara's anger at being without you.

Behind the patio door, a shadow paced or a tree swayed.

One of the young girls asked if I "know where Pop is?" I shrugged at her, noting the tomato stain around her mouth.

I tried to focus on the tiny girl, who speaks better than Benjamin and has the hard look of Clara in her eye. But the shadow was still there, and I couldn't. Something about speaking out of place and having done the wrong thing all along.

Clara told them you're "playing cops and robbers" and shifted her gaze to me. She hadn't been getting much sleep, she said. I could tell. She appeared less glamorous and mature than she had when I ran into her on the street.

Clara sent the kids to bed. She was eager to leave. Her tone was serious, and I wondered what difference there was from the factory floor to inside the home.

Clara applied lipstick.

We made Betty, who waddled like a canal mallard with child, stay inside with your children. They were supposed to be sleeping, but Betty said, "They ran the house." She called them animals.

Betty has become a figure of pity to all the women, with her husband on the front lines and her baby not yet born. It's become an omen—a pregnant woman with a man at war won't ever see her husband again except in the expressions of her newborn child. Betty has written him a letter and waits impatiently for a response.

It was chilly, so we wore our jackets when we stepped out the front door into the heavy smell of tomatoes. We ducked around the corner. Betty's sister was the loudest and could've made us detectable, though a prowler would never expect us stalking him.

Betty's sister stepped on a rock that threw off her balance, and she fell in a bush, letting out a cuss.

Someone grunted from the direction of the backyard. Probably a student from The Normal School trying to give us a scare. What was fear, anymore? There was a noise from the back again, and of course, I thought, he was goading us.

Someday, you'll return, and sit back there with your family, safe.

Betty's sister asked, "Who's there?"

The prowler took off toward the tomato lot, just where I imagined he would.

Clara, of course, being the lightest and fastest, was on the prowler's trail. Betty's sister, the slowest, came after us.

By the time we reached the tomato pile, the prowler was on the other side, crouching, I suspected. So, I picked up a tomato—heavier with water and seed than one would expect—and hurled it into a shadow, a silent assault.

It thudded, but I couldn't tell what it hit, and at that point, we could be throwing tomatoes at dogs or squirrels or stray cats. Or a headline: QUAKER MAID TOMATO PROVOKES PROWLER. I picked up another and dented the tomato's flesh with my fist. From the side of my vision, I saw Clara, looking just up the hill at the cemetery, where the prowler likely had darted.

"Damn it," Clara said to Betty's sister, her arms moving wildly about her head. "Couldn't you have been more careful? We almost had him. Jane," Clara said, turning to face me, "you're good at getting after men. Why don't you chase him?"

Betty's sister apologized profusely, referring to Clara by name, putting her arm on Clara's shoulder.

"You make me seem crazy! Leave me be," Clara said.

In my hand, the tomato was hard, heavy with the near-fall air. I wound up, and I'd never played baseball, not even in recess, but I would have been good at it.

After I launched, I heard the loud smack of a ripe tomato on Clara's crisp cheekbone. Clara howled. It echoed.

I nearly felt bad. Nearly.

I didn't go back to your house and probably <u>won't ever</u>. I watched from my window while Betty and her sister walked home, arm in arm, the two doors to their house, and every once in a while, Betty's sister gave out a hoot, one arm gesturing like a pitcher. Betty traveled by her side, belly casting a shadow round as the moon, against the street.

I went back out to see the shooting stars. The Cold Storage hummed all night long, and I felt safe with the night-shift workers inside. I stared alternately at the sky and the tomatoes we would can in the coming days, tender and vulnerable in the night air. Someday, they would be overseas at the war in a camouflaged ketchup bottle.

Before bed, Clara probably washed the tomato from her face angrily and harshly, pushing the Ivory soap further into her pores than needed, a seed clinging to her nostril. So lucky to have what she does, the forgiving love of her family no matter the wrath she sets upon them.

The clear sky's too vast and panics me. It goes on for so long my mind wanders out with the universe, wrapping the whole world in its black blanket.

A man's shadow cast tall and wide on the factory, and from where I sat, I pretended it was you, thought what I would tell you. Certainly, <u>I wasn't trying to kiss you.</u> How can I tell you all the things I want when I don't know, myself?

The shadow paced on the other side of the lot. Clara's right, the prowler exists. He stopped, stared at me for a minute, or maybe in wonder of the tomato pile, dawdling home.

Orient Express

"Mother?"

A hand falls on Cindy's shoulder. Before all this, Sandra would have called her 'Ma.' Cindy turns around. There she is. Her hair, short and dry, brass-blond, and unkempt, and her eyes, far-off.

"Sandra!" Cindy's breath catches in her throat and her nose stings. She's as unprepared for Sandra as she's always been. Her instinct is to back away, but Sandra grabs Cindy's arms and hugs her. When she pulls away, her daughter smiles, not how she used to, restrained and closelipped, hiding some big secret, but broadly, now, her teeth brag.

"Mother!" Sandra says, again, finally, as though begging her mother to talk. "What do you think?" Sandra asks.

"You're so skinny," Cindy says. "And your hair." She reaches her hand up to touch what once was silky and youthful. "Are you okay?"

"Aren't I? I'm so happy, Mother," Sandra says.

Her nails and cheeks have shadows of dirt. Her clothes smell like a hamper. She looks tired.

"You look like you need a shower and a meal," Cindy says, and Sandra acts as though she doesn't hear. She runs her fingertips across her eyebrow and yawns. Before, she would have flipped her mother the bird or told her to screw off. Perhaps the cult worked the skepticism right out of her.

Cindy opens the doors for her daughter, speaks up to the hostess first, and tries to be gentle.

She can't remember the last time the two went out to dinner together, alone, though their mismatched gazes and constant struggle of who orders first feels familiar. They both order breakfast though it's afternoon. It was something Charles, Sandra's father, always did.

"The canal has flooded in parts at home," Cindy starts.

"Where?" Sandra takes a bite.

"Eastport. The lock broke. The lake is too high, the pressure was too much," Cindy says. "It carried Uncle Robert's house right off the foundation."

"Oh, god," Sandra says. Cindy wonders what her daughter sounds like when she prays, and were Cindy listening, could she hear the sudden calm come over her daughter?

"We've all been advised to get flood insurance," Cindy says, holding this conversation like a rope from a cliff, and when Sandra doesn't respond, asks, "So what do you do these days?"

"We have busy schedules."

Cindy knows. Scripture readings. Selling candy or peanuts. Few hours of sleep.

"What do you sell?" Cindy asks.

"Flowers. Sometimes cashews. Little things like that," Sandra says.

"What do you do with the money?"

"Why do you ask? We give it to the team leader. From there it goes to Reverend," Sandra says.

Cindy dabs toast in yolk. "So, have you met anyone nice?"

"They're all nice," Sandra says.

"For God's sake, Sandra. Tell me *something*. Who do you stay with? Is anyone mean to you? Do you ever miss home?" Cindy lists these questions, wishing Sandra might respond one after another—satisfactorily, letting her mother know she would be okay. Giving permission for Cindy to go back home.

Cindy watches Sandra like she did when she was just weeks old, to be sure she'd breathe through the night: Sandra takes a long sip of milk, then she clears her throat, then she folds her napkin and dabs her lips. She scratches at a crumb stuck to the outside of the tumbler. The exhaustion creeps in.

"Sandra." Cindy snaps her fingers in front of her daughter's face.

"I stay in the compound, a ranch, not far from here," Sandra says.

"A compound? What, are you at war?" Cindy slips into her old habits with Sandra, the angry cuts and quips always somehow eased her own pain.

Sandra's smirk proves she knows what her mother is doing.

When Sandra was a baby, they lived in "Diaper Alley," a barracks-style housing complex between the railroad tracks and the university, where the roofs leaked and trains rocked the building. Sandra spent weeks with night terrors.

In the night, when Cindy would stare at Sandra's pinched, teary face in the dim light from the windows, Charles would mutter something about the war and roll away from Sandra's cries. Cindy pleaded with Charles to relieve her for just one five-minute walk, one moment to steal a cigarette or to have a drink with an old friend, anything to feel herself again, to consider the biology courses she abandoned to be a mother. Charles laughed at Cindy for crying over borrowed troubles—the tragic life she hadn't lived—when there were *real* losses stored in his mind. She felt silly having to justify her sadness, competing with a war veteran to feel anything at all. Her doctor prescribed her Valium, which she hid in her underwear drawer and took when Charles wasn't around.

One night, Cindy woke to squealing and cracking and the smell of something burning. Charles was on the roof setting off firecrackers, but ran up a poplar to hide. There was steam about the building, and the police coaxed Charles down from the tree. Sandra, in Cindy's arms, was too young to be anything other than hungry or fussy. Cindy watched her husband fall clumsily from the poplar and felt no edge of her seat, no quickening in her gut. Charles came home two hours later in a cast, and Cindy was relieved when he got into bed without speaking. All the stirring woke the baby, and it wasn't long before Sandra cried, as Cindy knew she would.

She wondered if Charles passed combat fatigue to their daughter.

Cindy watches life outside the diner window. Every town seems a replica of another. Bridgeport might be smaller, but it has everything this place has—diners, the theater, salons, cobblers, Moonies. Sandra hadn't had it rough. Parents die. So, Charles died belatedly in a house fire—their house, on fire. He'd always made it clear to Cindy he was on borrowed time he didn't deserve, and so now the fire became the belated end from the war he should have died in.

"Sandra, do you even remember what it's like at home?"

"Mother, the house is gone. Daddy is gone. Where is home now?" Sandra asks.

"Come back to Bridgeport, Sandra," Cindy says.

"I'm happy here, Mother. I'm God's soldier. We're all fine and safe."

"What a crock!" Cindy moves closer to the diner window and the warmth of the sun, watching Sandra ruffle her hair with her hand and the dust speckle in a beam of light. "Why did you leave?" Cindy asks.

"God called me," Sandra says, trance-like.

"That just isn't true, and you know it," Cindy says, playing the game the deprogrammer described to her: to act as though her daughter is under some spell. How easy it was for Sandra to turn to the cult without Charles and his madness alive to make her feel normal.

"He calls all of us at some point," Sandra says, growing insistent. Cindy's reminded of Sandra's teen years, when all a mother could do was wrong, when Sandra wanted more and more of the world and less discussion about the things she wanted. When Charles' career in gruesome forensic photography propelled him further into post-trauma and Sandra took advantage of the emotional turmoil. When Cindy felt caught between competing terrors and waited it out.

"Oh yeah? And how did he call you?" Cindy asks.

"Mother."

"Did you leave because your father died?" Cindy asks. Some days, when Sandra was growing up, Cindy created her own trouble with her daughter just to feel anything.

"You're being ridiculous," Sandra says, pushing her plate away.

That's it? Cindy thinks. Ridiculous?

The second half of this reunion, this "deprogramming," is, by suggestion of Mr. Theodore, something neutral, something where the two can just be in the same space together. Cindy knows she's messed up Mr. Theodore's first step royally. Sandra only grunts when Cindy asks if she's ready to go.

On Fifth Street, a man guides a shopping cart toward Cindy and Sandra. He wears a sack around his waist and is oddly buoyant—maybe a Moonie! Cindy waits for Sandra to say something or react, to give a hint this man is one of her kind, but she doesn't engage him.

At home, the Mayor of Bridgeport made a motion to block the cult members from soliciting to prevent any more college students from being lured in. The man has lost something besides an incisor tooth and his hairline.

After he passes, Sandra stops and turns to watch him.

"Do you know him?" Cindy asks.

"Who?" Sandra says, watching the man wheel his cart around a corner.

"That man. Who was he?"

"Let's go to the movie," Sandra says.

"Are you in danger, Sandra?" Cindy asks. If Sandra leaves the church, it wouldn't be unusual for the congregation to torment and stalk her.

One *Bridgeport Republic* article reported a former Reverend Moon follower a town over placed his head on an Amtrak railway just before the train barreled through. Cindy wasn't able stop herself from reading reports, from watching news documentaries. Reverend Moon won a Guinness World Record for the most marriages in one ceremony. It was on television.

Murder on the Orient Express is the only movie playing that Cindy has any desire to see. In the still of the dark theater before the movie begins, Cindy's already exhausted like the deprogrammer said she would be. He said it wouldn't be easy, but she has to fight for what she wants, and doesn't she, after all, want more than anything for her daughter to come home? And doesn't she? Does she?

"I wish you'd come home, Sandra."

"Do you?" Sandra asks.

The film's opening credits show news clippings of a kidnapping—a reimagining of the Lindbergh baby. The scenes are sporadic and dark and hardly make any sense, yet Cindy's nose burns as if she's about to cry.

Cindy stares for a moment at the flash of the screen on Sandra's cheeks. Sandra looks normal, and to everyone seated beyond their two seats, what's actually happening is not happening at all.

When Cindy told Sandra how Charles died, she tried to bend the facts, the brutality of it, but emphasized Charles probably died from the smoke fumes, not from the skin-melting, organ-burning, perishing of home. When it happened, Sandra was in class at the university and Cindy was at Scranton's Market. Cindy imagined Charles in his large leather chair watching the local news. Charles' afternoon cigarette dipped, suddenly igniting against the couch or the rug. He didn't suffer at all, Cindy told Sandra, though she'd known better.

"I'm going to the girls' room," Sandra says.

A moment after Sandra leaves, Cindy follows her and stands outside the stall, where inside, Sandra cries and recites scripture.

"May it be brought together again," she says.

For lack of a better place, Cindy looks in the mirror, surprised to see herself as entirely composed, her sensible skirt and buttoned blouse against the smells of antiseptic and toilet, the smoke from burnt popcorn. In the corner of the mirror someone has written 'I'm Watching You' in raspberry-colored lipstick.

"Who?" Cindy says out loud.

"Mom?" Sandra asks. Cindy imagines her shivering on the other side of the door but doesn't move.

"Sandra?" Cindy asks. How had she become so separate from her daughter?

"I'm okay," Sandra says, and continues praying. "When we are alone, we are never lonely." This is not a voice Cindy knows.

When Charles died, the house burned from the inside out quickly thanks to hoards of photographs, obsolete textbooks, the kindling that made up their lives. The fire department couldn't get it under control, and officials kept worrying Sandra was inside.

"I'll wait for you out here, and then we'll go get some water and fresh air." Cindy takes deep breaths and grasps the pill bottle in her purse. A crop of gray bugs speckle the sink counter like stealth fighters.

"No. Let's go finish the movie," Sandra says.

When they return to the theater, Cindy has lost all sense of where the film left off. On the screen, the train is stalled, and snow clouds the scene beyond the windows.

Sandra's eyes and cheeks flinch; it's as though her mind's gone haywire. On the screen, Lauren Bacall has a cigarette in a train car; her arm rests on the chair and the smoke trails upward. The thought creeps up without warning: Cindy wonders, were Sandra home with Charles that day in the fire, would she have been happier, safer.

Cindy grabs Sandra's hand, warm and calloused, and whispers, "I'll drive you back to the compound. I'll give you money."

Sandra excuses herself to the bathroom, and Cindy counts to ten, slowly, giving Sandra time to make up her mind to do whatever awful thing she will do next. The deprogrammer would tell Cindy she's earned her position as a mother without a child, and by the time Cindy cuts through the air of burnt butter and corn, the glass doors to the theater slam behind Sandra. She steps out onto the sidewalk and darts like a squirrel into traffic. Cindy stands behind the glass, watching. Horns ring out against the buildings. Her daughter runs down an embankment, her head disappearing beneath the horizon.

After the stoplight changes and traffic clears, Cindy steps out of the theater, onto the street, and crosses. Her deliverance comes in the last place she saw her daughter in motion, and there is nothing but trees, even when she sits on the ground and looks up.

Bittersweet Nightshade and Other Childhood Influences

I

Myrtle knew the corner of Barrier and Holley streets back when it was a skating rink, where she'd cracked her ankle one morning in the swirl of snowflakes. Her parents made her wait to go to the hospital, just a Victorian house on Main Street back then. They wanted to be sure it was broken, not just a growing pain, but by the next day, when the sun rose orange behind the steeple of Our Lady of Mercy, Myrtle woke to a throbbing ankle, swollen like a grapefruit but its color pretty plum. That morning's pain—having grown from unspoken neglect—became the reason why Myrtle would trip girls on the ice and then hug them, or vice versa. She blamed this for why her hugs were limp and few, why she couldn't love like normal people. When she neared thirty, she got pregnant. At nearly nine months along, Myrtle's mother walked her like a dog, fed her castor oil, and paraded her for blocks and blocks in the hard January air until she sat down to tie her shoes on the corner of Barrier and Holley and birthed her first son, Jerry, there on the curb.

Myrtle swaddled Jerry in hand-me-downs from older cousins and bathed him twice a day with lukewarm water until he was so clean he broke out in a rash. She fed him from her breast until others scoffed about it. The other kids teased him, but that wasn't what it was about, after all.

II

Back then, the library was on Canal Street surrounded by boxwood shrubs. Jerry walked to the Seymour Library on Sundays to renew the book *How to Draw Dogs*. He didn't have dogs. It never occurred to Jerry to own a living thing.

When he was in the sixth grade, Jerry took notes in Social Studies class. He wrote ravenously, whipping through the history of the world—the Qur'an, Buddha, the Roman Catholic Church. The last line of notes started off legibly, but by the time he finished it, the writing had gone rough and ragged, the ends of words nearly leaving the page, and there was a puddle beneath his desk. He sat while the bell rang, and the whole class left the room, and from there, the buses left the school, circling the campus roads, which were shaped like an ear. He looked at the teacher, then at the mess on his chair. She walked him down to the nurse after saying nothing, and her hands smelled like onions the way his mother's did after she made Sunday dinner.

His mother came to pick him up from school, and he brought his clothes home in a paper bag, the bottom wet by the time they got in the back door. She asked him, "What happened?" but he didn't know.

"Can we have a dog?" he asked his mother.

Embarrassed, Jerry skipped the next couple days of school, went to the library, where he sketched identical beagles one after another on a newsprint pad. The librarian's gray braid swung like a pendulum the whole day long, and she walked back and forth past Jerry, maybe pretending he was her son, but not asking how come he wasn't in class.

III

Jerry lived across the street from The Church of Changing Denominations. His friends were allowed all around the block, and they rode off without him, meandering around each other like vines. His mother told him there was nothing much around the block, as though he'd never seen it, but he knew the steep hill of Borden Street, the lure of the cemetery on Hill Street, the crash of the factories just beyond. There was a whole world beyond. Maples flanked the edge of his yard, and those were his boundaries. He rode his bike back and forth, turning around as soon as he gained any momentum.

Myrtle's husband was missing a leg from the knee down and wasn't useless, though certainly morose since the accident, drinking Genesee and listening to the police scanner. Jerry saw the accident happen from the sidewalk, and since had been drawing—first dogs, and now his father's missing limb, over and over. Jerry tried to bring home strays Myrtle sent away. Sometimes he stole other people's pets for an hour, but the owners always found him. The last dog he stole belonged to the neighbor who painted the steeple of the church the way Jerry had a year before the accident. After the man came for his dog, Myrtle and Jerry sat out in lawn chairs, watching the handsome neighbor reach upwards, casting his shadow against the building, painting white tufts either of them only ever saw in dreams, while Jerry's friends rode away.

IV

One day, when Jerry was twelve, he ate nearly a fistful of bittersweet nightshade berries he knew to be poisonous. He plucked them, one by one, at varying degrees of ripeness, and tried not to touch the leaves, which smelled. The smell clung to his fingers so many other days, like rye but worse—tart like grapefruit, but not as clean.

The berries were easy to chew, but the taste made them tough to swallow. The juice foamed quickly, the seeds like UFOs in his teeth. Before he knew it, the poison from the berries took over, and he finally felt fine.

He went for a walk around the outside of his house and saw the moon big as the hill in his backyard, though it was daylight. His father stood on the ladder across the street, painting the steeple and now had not just one, or two, but six legs, and told Jerry, "I am an octopus! I can paint with one hand, brace myself with the other, and still have six legs to stand on!" If Jerry were counting and not reeling, "*Six, not eight!*" he would have yelled up to his father while shielding his eyes from the bitter sun, which was then strangely close to the moon. But if he looked again, his father would not be painting the steeple, but asleep on the couch, dreaming of a life where he could walk—or run away.

Myrtle came running outside when Jerry passed his boundary—the stump where the maple once hovered in front of the Smiths' house. The last week a man dismantled the tree in the neighbor's yard, branch by branch, and Myrtle sat, sipping iced tea, watching from the stoop of her house next to the blooming magnolia. Myrtle's husband called out from behind the screened window, the static of the police scanner buzzing next to him and asked if the man could spare a stump. Next year, the magnolia would come down with a disease and not blossom, and Jerry's father would already be dead of a heart attack, and Myrtle would hide on her front porch, tired of these mini tragedies, these larger-than-life melodramas in which her son ate nightshade berries and, instead of dying, became as stoned as the college student who sold her Amway knives last spring.

V

When he was nine, Jerry watched in delight as his father reached under his bed and pulled out the brown shipping carton of firecrackers from Uncle Jack in Pittsburgh. When he opened the box, the sticks held all kinds of promise—energy released in a way that sent Jerry running to the middle of Church Street, giddy to watch air ignite.

The katydids were loud by the fourth of July. Tonight, his mother sat in the kitchen with the door open to hear if the police came by with cucumber slices on her eyes, a cigarette dangling from her lips and a cup of coffee near her elbow to appear uninvolved. She just wanted the house to herself, and supporting whatever shenanigans the boys got into this one day a year was fine enough for her. She did what she could to get by.

Boys' voices echoed off the brick Cold Storage down the street, which was, for Jerry and the boys of Church Street, the end of their world, so large it made whatever was beyond somehow not there at all. Jerry's father worked at the Cold Storage and wore a hard hat, which he wore that night to set off the firecrackers in the middle of Church Street. In ten years, after Jerry's father died, this detail came back to him while drunk, and he would laugh at his father for thinking that yellow helmet might have saved his leg.

What Jerry remembered about the fireworks that year, the last year he ever set them off, was his father let him ignite the wick with his Bic lighter, let him push the explosive into the galvanized pail filled with stones, the heat from the lighter's metal like electric to his fingertips. Jerry ran back to the sidewalk after lighting it, where his mother always made him stay, though she, herself, seemed somewhere else. Jerry's father was distracted by the neighbor's German shepherd who scavenged their trashcan, when the firecracker exploded.

Jerry could not see the colors of anything but dim and flickering streetlights and the illuminated firecracker—glorious sunspots in the dark —blown up to something so large it would last for years beyond the five minutes it took to destroy his father's leg. The stump of leg, which landed like a potato bug on the church steps, would stain the stone, as would the barrel-sized wound that bled fast on the slate in front of Jerry's home.

After, his father's whole life was drunk by fire—married to the horrors of the police scanner, the constant crackle of voices sitting next to him in his recliner. His father was asymmetrical, now, and symmetry was the only definition of beauty Jerry ever knew—at least until his father's heart seized, halting with mercy years later, but still ripe as nightshade in Jerry's mind.

Primal

The children of Church Street didn't know why police were canvasing house to house. Some parents might have been peering from their windows, having just closed their doors after saying they had no information. My parents were likely fighting and wouldn't let me outside. I watched from behind my mother's curtains as my best friend Leslie hid behind a large maple to overhear the officers, alongside James, a neighborhood boy we'd long considered our enemy.

Had someone gone missing? Had someone been killed?

By that time, Leslie found me unforgivable and passed my house to find anything else to do. I didn't understand my error at the time—children and parents were meant to live in separate worlds. In hindsight, if I were Leslie, I know, now, I wouldn't have been grateful a friend wanted to save my eleven-year-old life.

When Leslie stopped answering my knocks at her door, the horizon of Church Street stretched for what seemed like ever. And I can't pinpoint, now, how many days it was before my brother, too, left for good.

It began to rain as I watched Leslie and James go to their houses. The air from the Kleene Breez soap factory a street over sent suds down the gutters of our street. Then—a lull in my parents' argument. Cigarettes burning in their ashtrays. Mom in the kitchen. Dad in the living room. It was either the end of their fight or an intermission. The police gone from our neighborhood, excitement from the trauma expired. My stomach wouldn't settle until the next day, when my parents' voices calmed and their hands touched. Two cigarettes in one ashtray.

I sought shelter from my parents' arguments in my older brother's bedroom. It reeked of mothballs even then, before it became just a basement. And he was likely rolling a joint or curling milk jugs full of water when I made the slow descent to the basement, ducking for the low ceiling and watching the tricky stairs. The yelling picked up again, and I could hear their footsteps and voices above me, walking away from each other and then toward each other in a wicked dance.

The walls of the basement were covered with silver-lined insulation —the coolest room in the house. I could never have slept there. I sat on the bottom step and rocked back and forth waiting for the yelling to stop.

"What's it about this time?" Brad asked, fidgeting with a Folgers can of nails on my father's work bench.

"Got me. They won't let me outside."

"Where's Leslie? Why don't you sneak over there? I hear everything down here. Every. Fucking. Thing." He sat down on the step next to me.

I hadn't told Brad about Leslie. I held my breath and counted the seconds between yells like thunder from lightning.

"Some days, I actually listen to what they say, and it's pretty stupid, Josie." I didn't know, though. The fighting seemed to work for my parents. And the more my parents fought, the more my mother cleaned. Our house was always immaculate. If there was any love—sexual or affectionate—in my house, neither my brother nor I knew about it. For people who hardly stopped arguing, they could be mistaken for happy.

Up until then, I believed Leslie and I were different from the other kids on Church Street because our houses were clean, and our mothers made dinners most nights and drank coffee or wine. Or because both of our parents lived together in the same house, for better or worse. But after what I'd done, Leslie would walk past my house with James as though I no longer lived there, and their shadows would look like pulled taffy on the cracked sidewalks, stretchy limbs headed toward a funhouse.

Brad was smart. Besides, he was the oldest person I knew who would actually talk to me.

"Want to get out of here?" he asked. "Go get the umbrella. We'll walk."

A door slammed somewhere upstairs.

After every fight, my mother cried, and my father drove off with his Pontiac trailing some type of car fluid behind it. My mother would pop popcorn on the stove and let me do whatever I wanted so she could call my aunt to complain in peace. After my parents made up, they told me I was lucky they cared enough to yell at all.

That day on our walk down Hill Street, my brother told me about the murder.

The news story: she was folded in a refrigerator behind the rental property on Hill Street. But my brother told me the rumors—how a woman from Rochester named Natalie was raped, strangled, and the same cord was later wound around the refrigerator to keep her body inside, but her foot was wedged out the door, and that's how the landlord found her. My brother's hand moved frantically along with Natalie's story, punctuating the worst parts with movements that looked like charades or slapstick comedy.

We lived one street over from where Natalie's body was found, on the industrial edge of Bridgeport. Our neighbors were hardworking families, but our street increasingly lost itself to the crooked shutters of college rentals and dirt-laced lawns of family homes turned duplexes or triplexes.

There was the purple house, full of women with their young children and James, who was teased endlessly for being too old for middle school. My mother called James's mother and sisters *ladies of the night.*

And now James took my place as Leslie's confidant. My brother told me many times to lighten up on James, he was still a human being, and people like James were the ones who ended up running the world.

James constantly smoothed back clumps of his bleach blond hair. In hindsight, I see him as Kurt Cobain. He rarely talked. He was slow in how he walked and talked and probably how he ate or wrote his name. I bet he drew three-dimensional shapes on his notebooks and wrote dirty words in the margins.

Our falling-out began at the start of summer when Leslie tucked a short note in my hand. It was on pink paper from her parents' While You Were Out pad.

In the note, she referred to me as her diary, a strange metaphor since she rarely told me any juicy secrets, and up until then, I thought I'd witnessed much of her everyday life. How could I not have seen this part of her? We'd pinky-sworn on less-important secrets, like never to tell James we weren't really witches. And more importantly to me back then, we'd become blood sisters by picking scabs from scrapes and mashing the cuts together. We'd been friends since we were four.

Leslie had been at camp for a while, which had given me plenty of time to work my mind into a knot over whether Leslie would actually kill herself and what life would be like without her.

That night, when I'd heard Leslie's mother, Carla, yell out her kitchen door for her cocker spaniels, I went over.

"Carla!" I screamed from the back gate to the yard as if it were an emergency. I flipped the hasp of the gate and ran toward the house, where I could smell dinner. The yard was so green and their pool had turned green and everything around was lush and fertile and humid and all I wanted was to know Leslie would come back.

I was in the kitchen, having petted my way in via the dogs. One had a cancerous tumor and the other had hotspots that hurt to look at. I stood there, looking at Leslie's mother, debating what I should say and if I should just out with it, or what.

Carla was a painter, but she spent her days answering the phone at the village dentist. My mother called her bitchy because she never said, 'Hi.' She put fresh basil on her salads and let me pick snap peas from her garden. Her house smelled like earth, and her bathroom like Noxzema and St. Ives.

The glass of wine in her hand had lost its condensation. Chicken roasted in the oven. Everything my mother cooked was microwaved.

"Leslie's at camp still," she told me. "I can have her come by some time tomorrow, when she gets back."

"Carla." It felt weird to call a grown-up by their first name, but I didn't think talking to her like a teacher felt right either. I pulled the soft pink note from my pocket and handed it to Leslie's mother.

"What's this?" she asked.

It's not as though I can't imagine how this felt like a general betrayal of life in twenty years' hindsight, but at the time, I thought I was saving her daughter. I thought I was saving myself.

While Carla read, I regretted having come and moved foot to foot while I counted five bundles of lavender hung sporadically around the kitchen and then the brightly colored tea tins on her kitchen table:

English Breakfast, Chamomile, Earl Grey, Orange Pekoe, Oolong, Mint, Peach—Leslie and I brewed them all together in one large bowl before, tea stew, and nearly threw up at the result.

When Carla got tipsy or, as it happened that day, really angry, her Italian accent bloomed candidly from someplace private in her. Something cooking in the kitchen started to burn on the gas stove, and her eyes landed on everything but me.

"You need to go, Josie."

From then on, when I'd see Carla in her yard or walking down Church Street, she'd act as if I weren't there. And starting then, Leslie boycotted our friendship.

Some nights I'd stare out the small window in my bedroom while I thought questions to Natalie, like, *How is it to die?* and though the streetlights flickered every night for as long as I could remember, I'd decided it meant Natalie was flicking a streetlight switch in response to my questions, maybe she was saying, *Eh. So-so.* Then a Cold Storage worker would amble down our street after a midnight shift in faded Wranglers carrying a yellow hard hat and I would assume it was a sign he was the killer. I imagined him whistling a sad song.

By that time, my brother had run away, or maybe it was more like he just left, I don't know. But the day before my brother disappeared, he walked with me to Ames to buy a Ouija board with change he cashed in from the bottles he stole from the Owens-Corning factory. I'd worried out loud to him Leslie would actually kill herself. He'd told me sometimes people did that, like the guy who lived in the back of James's apartment that hung himself a few years back, and when people had their mind set on killing themselves, they would do it eventually. It was preprogrammed, he'd said, like a computer.

After my brother disappeared, I spent hours reading the *Time Encyclopedia* my parents ordered off TV. I looked up words like 'sex' and, after overhearing one of my parents' arguments, 'custody,' but there was no entry at all, and so I tried some random words I liked the sound of, like 'ephemeral,' but I only found 'epic.' When I found the word 'primal,' even to say the word began to scare me. Primal was the looming mess overhead. It was blood and man and rot. Food and body and anger. I looked up 'suicide.'

When Leslie finally answered my knock at the door, I knew it was only because she heard about my brother and felt sad or curious or whatever. Back then, people went missing and there wasn't an Amber Alert. My brother was eighteen. It wasn't even on the news. The community was not as concerned as I was. My parents were not as concerned as I was.

The familiar rush of lavender and eucalyptus came at me, and I felt like I could breathe again, yet, in Leslie, I saw someone I hardly knew, someone more sophisticated than I knew what to do with. She was tan, her freckles ablaze from the sun. She wanted to smoke a cigarette, and I wanted to use the Ouija board.

That afternoon, we sat with our backs against either side of the Seymour gravestone—I faced the red house where Natalie was murdered the month before, and Leslie faced the train tracks and the Kleene Breez Factory. The gravestones were dull, cracked pieces of Chiclet gum, and didn't stretch on as far as the prettier cemeteries.

After our cigarettes, Leslie and I were to begin the week's care for the Williamses' labs, a pet-sitting gig Leslie and I held a few times a year while the older couple vacationed. Of course, part of the deal was James, who Leslie asked for cigarettes, could follow along and check out the Williamses' VHS collection while we fed the animals.

Neither of us could see the other from our opposite sides of the gravestone.

"You see James yet?" Leslie asked, her head peeking around.

"Yeah, he's walking through the church parking lot," I said. Our old interactions would have me saying something like, "You owe me" or asking why she talked me into stupid things like smoking cigarettes. But by then, I needed anything.

"Hi, Josie," he said to me, lingering on the last syllable of my name.

"James," I said, and stood up, wanting to make the transfer of cigarettes as discreet as possible.

"Brought one for you, too, Leslie," James said. He wasn't holding the cigarettes like someone should hold a cigarette but wielded them like sticks to throw in anger.

James handed one to each of us and kept one for himself, which he ignited before passing me the lighter. I made a note of the way he cupped his hand though there was no breeze.

I drew in a breath of nicotine and the smoke fought its way back out. I imagined the cigarette to be a smudge of sage like the one I'd seen in an episode of *Unsolved Mysteries*, and worried for a minute my soul would be extinguished, and I looked at Leslie, too, who wanted to be extinguished. She inhaled hard and didn't even cough. Of course, we weren't extinguished, and so we stood there completely alive and burning.

The Williamses' house had plaques of dogs all over its walls. Mostly labs.

James wandered off until he stood in front of the Williamses' rows and rows of VHS tapes.

Leslie fed one of the many cats, and because I hadn't been over in a long time, the labs jumped at my waist and left paw marks under the elastic band of my underwear and then panted and whimpered at my knees while I finagled the sliding glass door.

As I set up the Ouija board in the kitchen, the dogs followed Leslie everywhere with their noses up her butt or in her crotch. Embarrassed for her, I tried not to look.

"A little girl named Emma died in my house, you know," I said, trying to set a mood.

Leslie sat next to James and said, "No way." They were so close, you could almost see the energy bouncing between them. My stomach ached.

"Way. My dad said she died of brain fever."

"How does he know?" Leslie asked. "My house is haunted, too," she said.

"I know," I said. We'd both heard strange noises we could have blamed on her pets if we wanted to. Her house was older than mine, a fact that struck me with envy.

"Leslie, didn't a man hang himself in James's apartment?" My brother had told me, like he always told me everything he knew, even if it was strange and skewed, and I thought about him, right now, sitting in the basement, only now he wasn't there, and I tried to imagine where he might be—a circus, a boot camp, Omelas, a friend's house—but I wondered if, right then, he was anywhere at all.

"Probably did," James said. "I hear things all the time."

I said, "My brother told me."

Mentioning Brad shut them both up and they squirmed. I'd known it was only a matter of time before Leslie would ask about him. But it would be on her terms.

James lit the candle with his lighter.

We sat in a triangle with our hands on the planchette. Leslie sat next to James, who'd become eerily serious. He was the type of boy who would grow up to work at the Cold Storage.

"Is anybody here?" I asked. We sat for a minute.

"Natalie?" I asked. "Are you there?"

James cleared his throat.

"Shh!" I said.

"Sorry," he said. His fingers went up toward his face.

"Stop moving," I said.

"Natalie, are you here?" Leslie asked. "Who killed you?"

"One question at a time," I told Leslie.

The collies paced around the kitchen, and the planchette sat still. I worried Leslie and James might get impatient.

I asked, "Is anyone here?"

We agreed it was my job to read the letters since I was the better speller, so when the planchette started moving, I leaned forward to read the responses. "N," I read aloud. "A."

Leslie burst out laughing.

"Are you doing that, Leslie? Come on."

"Sorry. I'll stop. Really," she said.

"Okay. Who's here?" I asked.

But she kept talking.

"None of us would have even known who Natalie was if she wasn't murdered," Leslie said. "How about your brother, Josie? You think he's here in spirit?"

"I don't know, Leslie," I said. "Maybe you could let me know if you see him when you get there."

The words come back to me all the time, as though I'd wished her to die. How I'd made it sound as if death were a place you could go and come back from, and when Leslie went just a week later, she didn't come back, and wherever my brother went, he never came back either. My parents said more about Leslie's death than my brother's disappearance, and to me, the only difference between the two was a corpse.

James and Leslie sat frowning with their hands on the planchette, and James looked at me in a scolding way, but didn't say a thing.

The planchette began to move, but now I was skeptical, thinking Leslie was sliding it with her fingertips. She'd ruined it already, but I leaned forward, and the planchette moved to "No."

The heat from the candle's flame warmed my chin until James and Leslie glowed with surprise.

Before they could say my name, I'd already grabbed the flames at the tips of my hair, pulling my fingers along the scorching strands. My fingers were black when I pulled them away, and all I could smell was singed hair.

"Whoa," Leslie said, her face red like it had been slapped.

I pushed the window open to let out the smell. The labs followed me to the bathroom where I rinsed the singed strands with water and Ivory soap, but all I could smell was charcoal.

Years later, I would wonder if I ever knew Leslie, or if she was anything other than my imagination—which was what my parents blamed for this or that. Like how after my brother left, the dishwasher door flew open in front of me. Or the time the television turned on by itself, to the Spanish channel, where I somehow understood the language. I was still young and knew these things could happen. I couldn't even see air, but I still breathed, so how could anyone be sure what was really all around us?

I could've been scarred by Natalie's murder, I could've been angry at Leslie and James and all the ugly life on our street, or how my brother left me without an explanation, and I'm still angry, even now, the internet can't find him. But none of it mattered then—and nothing without proof matters, now—which is the worst part.

Cold Storage

1

There were rows of babies, like a fully-stocked shoe store.

My last morning at the St. Barnabas Home for Unwed Mothers brought sick relief. I *had* to leave, but did I *want* to? To the nuns, each girl would be lucky to leave St. Barnabas without her baby—every girl came to the home in trouble, with her family's good name in jeopardy, and her future relying on this fact: after the baby was born, she'd make a clean break. She'd have the baby, recover, and then leave—grateful to have been given a "fresh start."

Just before the first feeding, at 5 am, when the babies were hungriest and loudest, I stood one last time, my back facing the windows to the nursery—the same windows prospective parents peered in to consider which baby they might adopt. I walked by on occasion while the couples, dressed in bell-bottomed slacks and cardigans or fishermen's sweaters, doted by the glass, like "How Much Is That Doggie in the Window?" a duet I sang with my mother what seemed like ages ago. When I returned home, it wouldn't be likely my mother and I would be reminiscing on sweet moments.

Last night, when I'd called my mother to say I was coming home, she told me a) she wasn't feeling well; plus b) in my absence, my parents, having been married twenty years, *finalized* their divorce; plus c) my boyfriend Daniel completed Basic Training and was now somewhere in Vietnam. Daniel didn't know about Baby Alice. He told me he was drafted and was sent off to Basic Training just days after I found out I was pregnant. I had no plans to tell him, so I took this timing as confirmation not telling him was the right choice.

There were myths a mother could pick out her infant's wail from a chorus of wailing infants by some twin-like instinct. Though this was unreal to me, I desperately wanted it to be true, so I tested this theory over and over. If the babies were crying in unison—as they usually did in the St. Barnabas nursery—could I tell which was mine? I'd only held Baby Alice, named after my mother, a few times because the nuns discouraged caring for your own child. And the longing I did or didn't feel for my baby, I'd blame on how my relationship with Baby Alice was regulated. If I woke in the middle of the night aching for her, I'd find myself complaining to Sister Josephine that I needed to see her more, and if I was tired of holding her after a minute or two, which was typical, I grew angry the other nuns disrupted our connection.

Motherhood *had* induced all kinds of strange in me: any baby crying would entrance me, and without realizing it, I'd rock back and forth as though I were soothing an infant. Sister Josephine and some of the birth mothers insisted this was a maternal instinct. Maybe it verified the bond between mother and child even after the mothers left their baby to some new, better, "more suitable" parent.

If the myths were true, I should know which of the tiny girls in the nursery was Baby Alice. Still, I mistook a Black infant's cry for my daughter's cry—and once, a boy's.

Sister Josephine came up to me a day or so after giving birth, and said, in my ear, "After you leave, you have thirty days before you have to sign the relinquishment papers. Maybe you'll change your mind." And then she'd squeezed my hand until my fingers stung. Sister Josephine always hoped the young mothers would keep their babies, which was against the instruction of the other nuns. Sister Josephine was beautiful and young, like she could be the other nuns' granddaughter. The older nuns talked about her with wistful pity, both missing the youth Sister Josephine had, and thinking her silly and naïve for being too soft, for putting her arm around us when she should have been scolding us.

Most of the mothers at the home admired Sister Josephine and wondered why on earth she'd joined the convent. I wanted to please her so much, after she squeezed my hand, I was nearly compelled to keep my baby because she thought I should. I wanted to make her happy, as though doing what Sister Josephine wanted would somehow make me good again.

Baby Alice was still pink in that newborn way. I watched babies lose their fuzzy skin and either plump up or thin out from their newborn weight, transforming, as though they knew what would be most appealing to shopping couples. I couldn't imagine bringing home a child like a sack of groceries.

Some infants seemed content even when cared for by nuns and mothers who weren't their birth mothers. So much for instincts. I began to think of returning home as leaving a group of unfortunate orphans instead of my own flesh and blood, perhaps because it was easier.

Just the day before, one mother, her belly finally bulging, watched a couple at the nursery adopt a child she'd cared for since she arrived at St. Barnabas months earlier. She had a fit, screaming and crying in the nursery. When Sister Josephine sent her back to her room, she fell quiet, and when she reached the stairs, threw herself down the thirteen-step staircase, belly first.

At St. Barnabas, I'd spent a lot of time in my small room. The room had one little window one nun discouraged me from looking out during the day, when the children of the orphanage were outside playing. Of course I watched longingly, but saw something wild and unruly in the children, some innocence in their flushed cheeks I would wreck.

There were corridors of unwed mothers, who—like the suddenly chilled infants who'd left the womb—knew something huge had changed, but unlike the infants, knew what that change was, and why it was, and it was the mother's charge now to forget it.

The morning I left, standing before the nursery, I wondered if it mattered at all who these babies were born to. I poked my head around the corner to see down the long hall that led to the front doors. I needed to be sure no one was coming before I entered the nursery.

Shaking, I slid the identification cards from the sleeves of each infant's crib, row-by-row, pocketing Baby Alice's, and threw all the rest into the air. Soon, the babies were startled with large scraps of confetti falling all over them, their identities thrown to the wind. I listened for the cry I thought could be Baby Alice, tried to string it out from against the others' cries. My nose stung with frustration and eyes watered at the last of all this, the way the pain both isolated and comforted me. When I thought I had her cry picked out, I memorized the gasps and rattling bellows, and without checking to be sure it was Baby Alice at all, I walked away.

2

I'd only been back from St. Barnabas one week when I woke to find my mother smoking a cigarette on the kitchen floor. Her legs weren't bent, but carefully straight, and at one knee was a can of Genny. My mother never drank alone, during the day—and beer, no less. The Genny, my father's favorite, must have been a remnant from before my parents' divorce, before the distance became more permanent.

My mother had looked better. For instance, she looked better when she woke up first thing in the morning with her mascara crusted under eyes and her hair cowlicked with sleep.

"Ten bucks if you can tell me what's wrong with my legs," my mother said. She extinguished her cigarette in the beer can. Charo, my mother's favorite breathing being, an unidentifiable brown mutt she inherited from a dead friend, lounged in front of her, a small brown mop of hair.

I bent down and looked in my mother's eyes. "Are you drunk?" I picked up the can. The beer was full, give or take a sip. And still cold.

"No, this was for pretend, to explain why I couldn't get off the floor."

Seven years ago, when I was ten, my mother was diagnosed with MS. At first, I only knew what I'd heard from Bridgeport's Red Feather Society fundraisers, about the committee leader's aunt and brother, people who were wheeled around or balanced with a cane, those who others were afraid to look in the eye.

For as long as I could remember, there were spans of time when it was my mother's habit to sleep until noon and then nap for two hours after dinner. This was how it was the week I'd been home from St. Barnabas.

"I can't stand," my mother said. "My legs feel gone."

I hoisted her up, and though she was tiny with little bird bones, it still felt like pushing a ten-speed through the mud. Charo lingered in the way, sniffing wildly at my calves. My mother's face grimaced from failed attempts at standing.

Years ago, the doctor warned us all extreme things like this could happen. This and many other things that would have been preferable and less debilitating, like a blind eye or numb pinky finger. I grew paranoid my mother would wake up one morning and not know who I was. Though the doctor didn't mention this specifically, I worried my mother would forget she had a daughter, she would have raised me all these years and then leave me as quickly as she'd loved me.

I let her go clumsily into a kitchen chair, but still felt her death grip on my skin. Unaware of divorce etiquette, I called Weber's, our family's convenience store, for my father to help. I knew it would have to be big to get him to come here, and since this disease was so fickle, for all I knew, she'd never walk again. So I described my mother's condition in awful terms—paralyzed.

"She's *what?*" my father asked.

"June, don't tell him. Don't bring him into this," she said. "Look at me!"

And so I looked at her because it was a reflex—I obeyed whether or not I wanted to. And then I left the room, stranding her at the kitchen table.

"Tell him to never mind," my mother called from the kitchen.

"She says to never mind," I said.

"I'm coming over," my father said.

"Sure. *Now* you are," I said.

Three weeks ago, I had labored for what the nuns told me was ten hours, though I only remembered a couple minutes of being scolded to breathe, and hardly. But that was when I was June *Landon*, a name the home gave me to preserve my identity, and now, it was as though I was the same person, but no one knew me anymore. Sometimes I didn't believe I'd had Baby Alice at all, though she crept into my mind when it was quiet—or sometimes when I'd touch my stomach, still soft and foreign, or sit Indian-style—and my muscles would recall her birth in little pinches and aches that made me gasp.

When the nurse said, "Don't push," I felt like I ought to, as if my muscles were running without me. It was the opposite of what anyone ever told me about labor. The minute I felt pain, the nurse administered so many drugs, I felt sleepy and nothing else. It wasn't long before my baby was crying, and now, just having lifted my mother off the kitchen floor, it seemed like something I'd done in a past life.

It would be, the nun said, as if it never happened. And to Daniel, my boyfriend, the father, it hadn't happened. Before I left, I tried to tell him, but my mother told me to hold off—dare I risk everyone in Bridgeport discovering the adoption? Then I worried, what would Daniel have done if he'd known? Made me keep it? Could he have?

My mother worried Daniel's family could have taken the baby away if they discovered I'd have it adopted, and I suppose it grew to worry me, too, to think I would be living in the same town as my child but no longer its mother.

Daniel was in Vietnam now, and I wouldn't have to tell him. It could be years before I'd see him again, and by then this would all be a memory. I'd written Daniel letters from St. Barnabas, and instead of writing St. Barnabas Home for Unwed Mothers above the return address, I wrote my name—my real name—as though the address were my cousins' house and made up stories about what I was doing in Buffalo instead of having a baby. I told Daniel I was babysitting—and in a way, I was.

The strangest-looking nun with the snaggletooth and pockmarks asked me if I was relieved to give my baby over to the Lord's will. What did that mean? If I decided to keep Alice, wouldn't that have been the Lord's will, too? Wasn't everything that ever happened in the world the Lord's will? My mother, only half-able to move, was that the Lord's will? Could what I'd done have influenced the Lord's will? Was it my punishment, now, to handle my sick mother?

Mother, pissed, folded and unfolded and refolded the placemat, wondered the logistics aloud while Charo napped.

"How do I get to the bathroom? Or to bed?" She always asked questions, but never truly wanted answers. Her worry always instigated my own anxieties. Sometimes it seemed as though she'd dream up things to worry about.

My mother picked at her lips, pulling at dry skin with her calloused thumb and index fingers, which was normal even though everything else was not, and then she flipped through *Redbook* aimlessly, probably because she heard my father come in the door and needed to focus on something. She always immersed herself in women's magazines and imagined she was amongst the many women in the ads with their neat homes and kitchen gadgets.

My father took his time getting to the kitchen. And when he did, my mother pretended not to notice him.

She pointed to the cover. "I always thought you could be on the cover of a magazine, June!"

"Every mother thinks their child could be something," I said.

That my baby would likely be in a stranger's hands, who knows where, if I didn't change my mind, made me wince, embarrassed—as though I never realized this was reality.

"Hi, Kiddo." My father kissed the top of my head.

"Oh, of *course*," my mother said. "Hi, Alan."

My father put his hand on my mother's shoulder and squeezed. He inspected her legs for injury, but would find nothing because they looked just fine.

"I come home, you two live in separate places, and Mom. Look at her," I said.

My father stood like he always did, indignant, but also pretending to be fine. I couldn't take on the thoughts of my father when my mother was the one who really had the battle. But I knew he had his own guilt about leaving her.

"Why don't you say 'Hi' to your dog, Alan?"

An instinct of maternal protection took over. "You should get rest, Ma," I said.

"Don't you talk to me like you're my mother, June. I am your mother," she said. "Everyone talks to me like I'm stupid. I'm not a child. I know what I'm doing."

Until now, my mother was mostly "fine." For years, when I noticed something strange, a limp in her step, a quivering hand, my mother always gave an explanation. She had never worked except when needed at Weber's and so was able to stay home and rest through it while scanning Black and Decker catalogues. Even at her worst, a severe case of vertigo, she was still a whole person who bought percolators for guests who never came and bedspreads for spare beds we didn't have.

Having passed the *Redbook* articles "I Hate It When They Call Me Ugly" and "New Easy-Care Child Clothes," my mother spent five minutes stalled on the article "Ten Secrets to the Perfect Marriage," snorting. She argued the feeling in her legs would return because when her hand went numb, it was only a matter of time before the feeling came back.

"Christ. Your hand went numb?" my father asked.

"It just fell asleep," my mother said.

"For how long? The doctor will do something. I'm calling," I said. The reality was, we were all reluctant to acknowledge the doctor could not do anything—I knew this from my mother's smaller challenges, but it passed some of the burden on to believe he could provide anything at all.

"Ohhh, leave me alone," my mother said.

My father meandered my mother to the sofa, where she wanted to nap. Charo hopped up on her legs.

"Just carry me back out of the house over the threshold, why don't you?" my mother yelled, swatting at him.

"Alright, Alice. Relax. Tomorrow's another day," my father said. Just last year, my mother's temper would have sparked a fire in him, but he'd seemed to realize her life now was beyond their petty fighting.

Growing up, I rarely talked to my father one-on-one. So now, discussing my mother with my father felt like an unfair alliance in which my mother fought her battle alone. Of course, I didn't think of my parents as two warring sides before the divorce. In fact, I accepted the many times they fought while I was growing up as bonding sessions. Not every man for himself, but all for one.

"Your mother is a hard woman to please, June," my father said. "I only wanted her to be happy, but at some point, failing to make her happy made me miserable. I spend my whole life failing. Look at all the stuff she has around here. She could shingle the house with placemats. Nothing I buy or say or do can make up for what she's missing."

She was curled under an afghan on the couch, and I knew I would be the navigator for any move my mother made after she woke. I wondered what my father wanted to succeed at. Love? Tennis? Being happy? Playing guitar? Who knew. I didn't know. Maybe he didn't either.

"What kind of baby was it?" my father asked. We'd hardly talked about the pregnancy, about St. Barnabas, as though that whole part of me existed in a gap between us, a place where it never touched him, so I was surprised when he asked anything at all. I was supposed to be forgetting.

"Kind?" I asked. "The baby was many *kinds*: illegitimate, white, unknowable, orphan, lonely." So many variables. "It was a girl, and I named her after mom, if that's what you mean."

"Sorry," he said. "Are you okay?"

"*I* can walk," I said.

Growing up, the fights between my parents made me sick.

My stomach knotted and I would run between the two of them, two all-powerful beings whose minds I was supposed to change about the other. At its worst, our German Shepherd would bark. I would cry, too. And if one swore at the other, I would run to the other to apologize for what the one said.

"Look, I didn't know the divorce would do this to her," my father said.

I didn't know for sure the divorce was a catalyst for my mother's decline, but it didn't hurt to let my father believe it.

"We agreed to it," my father said.

Agreed, so close to *agreeable,* positive, as though good for anyone. My mother was asleep and when she woke, she would not be able to shower alone. I tried hard to remember days when I was just a little girl, but even then, I was the older cousin who played dolls with the younger cousins. The hair-braiding, big-sister type who sliced the hot dogs and watched the kids while my mother and aunts sipped on wine.

"We haven't been happy—almost ever," my father said.

Thinking about it, I realized all of my parents' fights were categorized as "the worst" in my mind. Though they fought, the possibility of divorce never entered their vocabulary. It seemed a cross to bear that they stay together.

3

When Daniel and I first started dating, we met at the outskirts of the Cold Storage parking lot at night, in the shadows of the Birdseye tractor-trailers.

"She told me she thought she was dying," I said to Daniel. That night after dinner, I had witnessed my mother's first severe relapse.

Now, safely away, I was on my back in the grass by the rundown, red-shingled rental at the end of Church Street. Daniel had my head in his lap, tying loose knots in my blond hair.

"Do you think she's dying?" he asked.

He wasn't always the best person to talk to—he had experienced death in a way I hadn't, had watched his father's slow suffocation from lung cancer. This also made him alluring to me, knowledgeable in a way that scared me.

That night, before the ambulance brought my mother to the hospital, she sat like a snail on the bathroom floor, her head tucked between her knees, turning to vomit into the toilet. When I tried to pull her up to go to bed, she couldn't stand without falling.

My father was at the store and had been gone since he and my mother had a monumental blowout the night before, so I called an ambulance.

I had watched, my hands over my mouth, until my mother asked me to place my hands on either side of her head to keep her from flipping over. Then my mother heaved into the toilet while I held her hair in my fists.

Vertigo, the doctor had suggested in the emergency room later that evening. While I explained all this to Daniel, his face was so serious it panicked me. I sat up.

"*Is* she dying?" Daniel asked.

"We're all dying," I said.

"Don't be a ditz," Daniel said. "What's your ma doing now?"

I liked that he cared to ask questions and the possibility he could help me figure out answers. "Sleeping at Canalside Hospital," I said, but I didn't know for sure. Maybe she had woken and was staring out the window at the Erie Canal, wondering, like me, what would come of her.

"Come with me," he said.

Just on the other side of the industrial yellow gate was Hill Street, a dead-end street, and the Hill Street Cemetery.

"Funny it's a dead end with a cemetery and a cold storage," Daniel said. "You afraid to die?" He shoved his hands in his jean pockets and kicked the black gate of the cemetery.

"Afraid my mom will," I said. Daniel was seven when his father died. Everyone in our high school had known and was reminded when he pointed at the sky after scoring in a soccer game. When we realized his father had died, we all treated him like a celebrity, and losing his father gave him power as if he'd mastered something we hadn't, and hopefully wouldn't, for years.

"You get by," Daniel said. His scruff and his declared wisdom made him seem older. His long reddish hair stopped just short of his jaw. We both had just graduated from high school. I would begin my English degree at SUNY Bridgeport that August. Daniel wanted to work for his Uncle Gary's construction company.

I often wondered what Daniel remembered from age seven. It was obvious his mother doted on him since his father's death. She ironed—down to the underwear. And their cupboards were full of baking soda and cream of tartar and things my mother wouldn't know how to use if she had to. Daniel's mother made homemade peach pie. She was a member of the Red Feather Society and raised money for multiple sclerosis, a fact I felt horrible for resenting. Daniel's mother drove a car, which my mother stopped doing after her accident. I imagined his mother saved slivers of his nail clippings in a scrapbook somewhere, and this turned me off, thinking his mother had already established an obsessive trench around him.

Daniel left me on the crumbling sidewalk and went into the cemetery.

"It says not after 6 p.m.," I said.

"It's fine," Daniel said. "We'll just tell the cops we're visiting my pop's grave if they ask. No one ever comes here anymore."

I followed quietly, as though every moment spent in a cemetery ought to be somber. I stared at a gravestone with a last name I recognized from school. Daniel had walked to the back of the cemetery, near the little stone building I supposed held the maintenance tools.

I walked to catch up with him. Bodies under stones, was all I could think. On the other side of the chain-link fence at the back of the cemetery was a railroad track with hardly any traffic, and beyond, the old Quaker Maid Factory, where my grandmother died of a heart attack years and years ago.

When I came up to him, he put his hand on the space between my collarbones. We hadn't had sex yet. I was still a virgin.

"Life isn't as fragile as you think. Hold your breath," Daniel said. "I dare you to hold your breath until you pass out. You can't do it. It takes a lot to kill a person."

This was something I'd done before while driving past cemeteries, though it was holding my breath until I passed a white house, and just a game I played with my cousins, but here, inside a cemetery, and envisioning my mother balled-up with her eyes closed, already made me feel as though I was holding my breath.

"I'm not doing that, you weirdo," I said.

"Come on," he said, holding his hands out at his sides. "Your mother won't die from this. And you won't die even if you do watch your mother die."

"When I was in kindergarten, the bus would drive past the cemetery, and I believed everyone went to the cemetery to die," I said. "I sometimes worried the bus would make a stop here."

"Dying's not as neat as an appointment." He slid two of his fingers beneath my belt loop and pulled me over to him, which made me forget how he acted like a know-it-all.

We sat on the grass beneath the young trees that grew up through the chain link fence. I couldn't even remember kissing Daniel that night in the graveyard. I wasn't afraid of being caught, of anyone seeing us. I was hungry enough for some kind of break from my mother, some way to reclaim my life, I didn't care enough about a respectable place to have sex for the first time.

4

To get to Bridgeport University, I went out of my way down Holmes Street past Daniel's house, like someone shy to eat a meal even though they're voracious.

I understood after my mother explained why he couldn't respond to my letters, that he had left Basic Training and the address I'd received from his mother was no longer good. I was relieved he didn't receive the letters, and even more so he hadn't read them, because though I'd lied in the letters, it wasn't technically a lie if he never read the words. I couldn't have told Daniel I was having his baby at St. Barnabas if I'd wanted to.

Daniel's house, the stupid trashcans, his mother's old station wagon and the bundles of *Suburban News* stashed in the corner of the small porch made me wish he was home. I fought the urge to visit his mother, who, I imagined, would be alone inside doing something wholesome only good mothers do, like baking piles of shortbread cookies, Daniel's favorite, without him home to eat them.

I'd witnessed every one of my mother's struggles for the last three days. My father hadn't been over since the afternoon he'd carried my mother to the couch.

It was a chore to deal with someone who didn't want to be dealt with. My mother hardly wanted to speak. I hardly wanted to speak. The only words that passed between us involved awkward maneuvers to the bathroom, making her meals, and finding reading material. Occasionally, we took turns crying. Neither of us had anything to offer as a consolation to the other. It was as though we were grieving something similar but in entirely different places. Our coffees went cold, our olive loaf sandwiches went half-eaten. Finally, I promised myself I would walk to the university while my mother napped, to re-enroll at Bridgeport State University for the coming fall semester.

When I came upon the peace rally outside Heddon Hall, I recognized a boy from before I'd left to have Baby Alice.

"June!"

Last fall, ages ago, while most of the poetry students wrote poems about the war, Tom wrote the best poems about the war, poems without exclamation points that were posted all over campus buildings as protest.

He'd explain the Heddon Takeover was soon, and he was circulating recruitment fliers.

When I left for St. Barnabas, I never thought anyone would notice I was gone, especially Tom.

"How's the war protesting?" I said, nodding at the stack of posters in his hand.

He shrugged. "You coming back?" he asked.

"On my way to the registrar, now, actually."

We walked to the Rainier Building, catching up on the world that happened while I was at St. Barnabas.

"Wanna have a catch-up drink with me at The Cellar?" Daniel asked.

I would have never considered having a drink at a bar with another boy if Daniel were home and not in Vietnam, and now, what were the rules about our relationship?

The way Tom was standing—two feet away, casually and platonically, his hands full of posters—seemed harmless, and it seemed normal, in my abnormal life, to go with him.

"Sure," I said.

When I got there, I had nothing I wanted to talk about. The world was exactly as I knew it was—alive and happy and going on without me. Tom moved easily past the small groups of people, lit by pendant lights and neon signs, greeting everyone he knew, and my instinct was the opposite, to hang on the fringes with my sweater folded over my arm, but I let him pull me along.

Tom put his hand on my shoulder to move me toward a booth. It felt nice to be touched when the person touching me didn't need me to keep from falling.

The conversation started slowly, and I realized how long it was since I talked to a boy, though I wished I didn't have to be so careful to reveal the life I'd just lived.

"Your family lives around here, don't they?" Tom asked. He took a sip of his beer. "It must be great to get some grub and have laundry service and everything right here, when you need it," Tom said.

I nearly laughed, picturing my mother asleep on her side of the bed, her quiet snore she insisted she didn't have, the five o'clock news flashing updates from Vietnam on the screen in the corner.

I hated the taste of beer, maybe something learned from my mother, but I drank it today anyway, stifling the sour face I would have if my life were mine anymore.

"Where you from?" I asked, relieved to realize I knew nothing about him and this could take up the remainder of our conversation.

Tom's parents, both teachers, were still married and present, as in, aware of the world around them and able to care for themselves. They were supportive of Tom and his "flaky poet ways" that led him away from Newark. Forget sharing with Tom that my mother couldn't pee without me accompanying her to the bathroom. Forget that I bathed my mother (baths my mother had to be coerced to take in the first place), and I saw the red-blue veins on her legs and the embarrassment on her face, which I shared, when I helped her remove her underpants.

I became frustrated by the number of times he asked about my life, the number of times I had to re-route the conversation. I missed how Daniel knew my troubles and had seen so much unfold. I hadn't had to explain anymore. More, I wanted to be wanted, not needed.

"What do your parents do?" Tom asked.

"We own Weber's, the convenience store on Merchant Street," I said, lumping my mother in with "we," though she'd become so far outside of the "we." For all the work she became, she'd also become invisible, a pile of work, a terrible thought. Sometimes, I wanted to reduce my mother to something I could hide in my pocket to keep safe company.

"Oh God," I said, wishing I had a watch to look at. "I've gotta run. I told my mother I would make dinner."

"Want me to walk you home?" Tom asked. He seemed startled and curious, worried he'd said something wrong. I walked a thin line of wanting something I shouldn't have. I wanted Tom to take me from my mother and her body, now two separate things to me.

"No," I said, quickly, to be sure there was no question. I would walk home to avoid having to explain anything—the strange new boy to my mother, or my strange mother to the new boy.

5

Nearly a year ago, when I told my mother I was pregnant, we were in Weber's helping my father close up for the night. Weber's smelled like Pine-Sol and Smarties, and when the store was quiet, the fluorescent lights hummed and what the light touched appeared unnatural.

I sat at the counter, refilling the candy jars while my mother counted the till.

Every once in a while, my mother would lose count, say, "Dammit," and then start again. I remember thinking I could have counted it three times already, but I didn't want to be caught in one of my mother's webs of suspicion, like when a frying pan or a Pyrex bowl was nowhere to be found, should she be convinced a five or a twenty went missing. I let her keep going.

To me, the pregnancy seemed a non-issue until I said it aloud. Sort of like death—you knew something awful was coming, but when it was so far away, you found it easy to be distracted until it grew quiet enough for it to reappear.

The mindless task of counting the Mary Janes did that to me that night, the repetitive rap of one candy against the others. The clock said quarter to nine, fifteen minutes to closing, so I was antsy to get out, to walk around the corner to our house and read until I fell asleep, which was all I wanted to do those days.

I couldn't get past the unfortunate promise of childbirth. I feared the ripping pain that made me blame the baby for growing inside, and worse, made me hope I'd lose the baby. Or better, maybe my parents would be mortified enough—I'd put my money on my father—to suggest I get rid of the baby the way Margie Stevens did. Everyone knew about Margie Stevens.

"Suppose Daniel got me pregnant," I said.

My mother set the dollar bills down. The look on her face began as one I never saw before, and changed by the second, like a TV with its dial turning. At that time, my mother had already lost her sharpness and I often wondered what she thought about. She never talked about current events like my father did. Most of the time, when my mother spoke it was out of complaint. Anytime I would say something benign that didn't require a response, my mother would say, "Not now, June, I can't concentrate on what I'm doing."

That night, I thought maybe I'd broken her because she actually seemed to be processing what I said.

"June," my mother finally said. "That wouldn't be so bad!"

"I can't have it. I don't want it," I said.

My mother tilted her head, leaned in, and lowered her voice. "Oh, June. Don't be scared. Of course, it would be complicated and hard, but we would help you. Your father and I."

Her expression was unaware of itself. Her face did whatever it wanted without her permission. Eventually her face landed on a smile. And I should have seen this coming, my mother always wanting more and more of anything and everything, and how changes were just good things to make my mother's life different and satisfying, even when satisfaction never came. And before my mother knew it, she'd been in a twenty-year marriage with a bedspread collection that grew by the month and five sets of dishes, two of which were white.

I imagined another child around, an innocent person to be soothed. Another voice in the arguments.

"And you'd better let me tell him," she said, shuffling single dollar bills in her hands.

"Tell me what?" my father asked. He came out from behind a Little Debbie display. His hand caught between his hair and his eyebrows as he closed his eyes.

When the last two customers, young boys, came up to the candy jars, I stepped away from the counter and let my mother take control. I pushed a butterscotch tab around in my mouth until the candy slivered the roof and I tasted blood. The boys plucked candies from each jar, one at a time, their loose change smattered on the counter. How simple it was to be a boy.

"Get home now, boys. It's dark," my mother said to the kids.

The bell on the door clunked against the glass.

Watching my mother explain the pregnancy to my father felt a little like being five again, when I was invisible behind the screen door of the porch, watching my parents discuss a family drama.

My father asked, "How does this shit even happen?"

"Alan," my mother said. "Let her be. We can handle this!"

"Who's we? You're out of your mind," my father said. "This is a nightmare. We don't all live in La-La Land where everything is fine, Alice."

The look on my mother's face made me feel like I was crazy for not wanting to keep the child. That, naturally, the baby should be raised in the very same house I grew up in.

"Shh—Don't you know a baby is a blessing? It can hear everything you're saying right now," my mother said.

My father put his fist down hard on one of the shelves and my mother rested her palm on my stomach.

6

My mother was on the telephone when I arrived home, moving her right index finger along the account number of her Diners Club card as she read it aloud. When I walked in, my mother shrunk back. Was it shame? Embarrassment? Fear? I made a mental note to put my mother's credit card out of reach the next time I left.

Though the house felt changed, and half the contents I would have recognized as my parents' (a single unit) had disappeared, the amount of stuff in the house managed to multiply. Each day brought a new shipment—a gold clock for the family room (could she still call it a family room?) that gonged every quarter-hour, a set of four plush towels and bathmats, and shiny, unblemished pots and pans my mother would not be able to stand at the stove to cook in.

I didn't keep house the way my mother did when she was healthy, and so the space immediately surrounding her, the dining room table, or sofa, or her nightstand, was always neat, but the parts of the house out of her reach gathered clutter and crumbs and newspapers, and I caught my mother's scoffs when I walked past a mess without tidying it.

My mother hung up the phone and pointed to a knick-knack on the buffet table.

"What do you think?" she asked.

"What is it?" I asked. We considered the thing from across the room —an animal of some sort—iridescent and matching none of the décor in the house. "Is it a bull? Or a reindeer?"

"It's a nutcracker," my mother said. "You don't like it? I like it. You don't?"

"It's okay, but do you need it?" I asked. I sat down next to her.

"I didn't have a nutcracker," my mother said. She flipped a page in the catalog she just ordered from, squinting into the items like essential information, and I tensed in hopes she wouldn't find another item to order, like a new sewing machine, since she didn't sew.

"But you also don't have a Ferrari," I said.

"I'm not allowed to drive," my mother said.

"Never mind," I said.

The *Service News* section of the paper was on top of the mail pile that had grown in the past two weeks.

"Did you see Daniel's name in there?" my mother asked.

It wasn't an obituary. Daniel's assignment: Cambodia. The next column over detailed missing servicemen and deaths, which were growing and more than likely the same thing. "Cambodia," I said. I tried hard to imagine him off at war. On the surface, I knew, but when I tried to picture it, I only saw images of toy guns or Civil War photos from history class, and nothing real enough. Instead, words and my desire to put them in order wrestled me for reality. Slowly, Daniel took on different modes of life and death, and to picture him, to wonder about a conversation we might never be able to have, became impossible.

I shifted away from the paper and picked up a catalog. *General Hospital* buzzed in the background.

"What about the baby? Are you to going St. Barnabas to sign the papers? Or to get her?" My mother didn't mean this as a question.

It didn't surprise me she'd already forgotten what I'd told her the other day, like she forgot her lit cigarette on the dining room table—that I was going to sign the relinquishment papers. Was it wrong I couldn't believe I had Baby Alice at all, let alone held her. Did I even know for sure she was a girl? By the time I worked backwards enough, I didn't have to go back to St. Barnabas to sign anything for anyone.

But I humored her, as a parent. I had a responsibility in Buffalo, which remained my responsibility unless I signed some stupid paper. "I'm not getting Alice. What could I do to make her life any better than real parents could?"

"Real parents? What are real parents? Some people might call the actual mother a real parent, not some pocketbook," my mother said. "And what if *I* adopt her? You can help take care of her, like a big sister."

This fear lingered in my mind ever since my mother whispered when they left me at St. Barnabas on the last day of my life as I'd known it, *What if I raise the baby?* and since, I'd felt hostage to the worry my mother would resurrect this bizarre option.

The phone rang. I hoped it would be Tom. It would be Tom if my mother got it at the second ring, I wagered. I wanted him to steal me away from this.

It rang again, and my mother answered it. I listened to her new clock tick, and then chime, waiting for her to hand me the phone. Under ten seconds, it would be for me, but over ten seconds, it was something else.

"Declined? That's not right. I'll call my husband to see if maybe he gave me the wrong card," my mother said. My father told me he was canceling the credit card no matter how bad he felt she was falling apart.

Her face reddened, and I grew warm with her embarrassment, how she panicked and blamed her "husband." The bull-elk-nutcracker glowered from the table amidst ceramic owls, glass seashells and crocheted doilies. It was too much to look at.

After she hung up, my mother's face contorted and this meant she would cry hard. Her worst tears came from failure or shame, and I moved to put my arm around her, but she pushed me back. And was she able to, I knew she would walk out.

7

A week or so later, Tom asked me to join the Heddon Takeover movement, and I considered telling him about Daniel, how I prayed for him every night even though it wouldn't do any good—like having a convict endorse you for president. And when Tom put his hand on my leg, my boyfriend was in Cambodia, a place I'd only come to know through them both.

Outside the Scranton's Market, where Tom and I spent hours each night talking on the curb of Canal Street, away from my mother's house, he almost kissed me. I tried to transpose some memory of Daniel's face over Tom's, but my insistence it actually was Tom, my desire for it to stay Tom, made me pull back.

"I had a baby," I said to Tom. Saying it felt like a sick stomach, like when you make up your mind not to throw up, but then, you can't control everything with your mind, and those parts of your body take off without you, like I tried to hold Baby Alice in, keep her from separating.

"Holy shit," he said. "You don't have to lie, June. I'll back off."

"Not lying," I said, surprised at how matter-of-fact I could be.

"How am I supposed to believe that?"

"You think you know everything about me? You don't know everything about anything."

"Alright, where is it, then?"

Why did people talk about infants like pets, I wondered, calling them "its," asking what kind? So I told him where I'd really been. Why I never had anything much to say about last fall. And the more his face looked hurt, the more I told him, and the more wounded he looked, the more I kept going and going until he nearly cried.

Tom asked if I was going back to get Baby Alice. And even though he'd hardly believed me when I told him about the baby, it wasn't long before he acted as though keeping the baby was plausible, sensible, and expected.

"So, what will happen to her?" Tom asked.

I thought about how I'd taken her ID card and wondered what the nuns did to identify the babies, if they cared enough to do it at all.

"She'll be adopted by someone who can raise her right," I said. The market we sat outside was closing, and women in aprons walked to their cars, giggling.

His hand was on mine the whole night, but was not anymore. Suddenly, I was someone's mother. "It's been three weeks since I left," I said. "And I'm not bringing her back here."

He never asked about Daniel, and I never told him about where he was or what he was doing. There was no place I could go where my baby didn't exist.

One day, Sister Josephine allowed Baby Alice into the nursery while the others were out.

I held her, knowing this was the closest I'd ever be to my daughter.

Baby Alice woke up while I was holding her, and stared at me with doll eyes, wider than marbles and blue-gray like all newborns' eyes were blue-gray, and like she knew I would leave her behind. Who knew what color they would become? She started to cry, and that's when Sister Josephine came over and took her away for feeding.

"If you come to the Heddon Takeover with me, I'll drive you back to St. Barnabas to sign the papers," Tom said.

8

The night of the Heddon Takeover, my father pulled in the driveway just as I peered out the window, looking for Tom.

"June-bug!" my father called, pushing a wheelchair up the walkway. "Do you have any idea how much these things sell for?"

I knew what my father was up to. I could hear him now, after I called him for help with my mother, and he hung up the phone, cursing out the fact he had to "take care of Alice," who now rebelled even harder against her disease. She'd started doing stretches and exercises using her upper body, and her mood, though sometimes still angry, sometimes resembled hope. My father was probably frustrated divorce now ultimately meant an end to nothing.

"Oh, you'd better not bring that in here. No sir," my mother called through the porch screen. The wheelchair was burnt orange with a hole in the vinyl and didn't look sturdy enough to hold a person. And Tom would be by to pick me up to go to the protest any minute. My mother's position in her wicker chair on the porch wouldn't do anything to hide her paralysis from Tom if the wheelchair was hanging around.

"It was a steal at Thriftmart!" my father said.

"Secondhand goods?" asked my mother.

"Come on, Alice," my father said. "Lighten up, will ya?" He'd called me to see what she needed, and I thought maybe if my mother were paralyzed my whole life, he'd have been gentle.

My mother woke that morning unable to see out of her right eye. She sunk into the couch, covering her face with a pillow, so I thought she would be safe there for a while. Though when I walked back to the porch to offer my mother some English Breakfast (her doctor recommended less coffee), she tried to pull her legs behind her with her arms extended. A trail of magazines and knick-knacks splayed at her sides.

When I called my father in tears, my mother yelled from the floor of the porch, "Don't listen to her, Alan. I'm fine. She's got the baby blues!"

Instead of my father, I was now listed as the emergency contact on my mother's medical forms, which meant whoever found my mother in a physical disaster—say, at the bottom of a flight of stairs or unknowingly crossing when traffic wasn't clear or losing her ability to speak—would call me, and then I, not knowing what else to do, would call my father. Now, my middle position was documented.

Tom walked up the sidewalk, smiling. He wanted to meet my parents and looked almost gleeful it happened without having to seek my permission.

"Newspaper boy?" my father asked, gesturing to Tom.

My father's jokes always required apologies or explanations, and now, he seemed lighter, as though his burden had flown away. He was no longer my mother's only means of staying afloat.

"Tom. June's friend," Tom said. He held out his hand.

I refused to bring friends around my parents. For this reason.

I turned my back, attempting not to be mortified. I counted the tops of the pines peeking from behind the roof of our house.

"Thomas!" my mother said as though she knew him.

"It's Tom," I said.

"Tom, do me a favor, will you? Will you take that wheelchair to someone who needs it?"

I told Tom about my parents, how they welcomed any newcomer to the family by placing them directly in the center of their arguments. But I hadn't told him my mother couldn't walk, and with her messed up syntax, even her small talk left people confused.

"Ignore her," I said.

"Alice, just keep it around in case your daughter doesn't come home one day. Tell her, Timothy, nothing lasts forever," my father said.

"His name's Thomas," my mother said.

Tom's eyebrows were raised, and he tried hard, I could tell, to hide his surprise about my mother's paralysis. He worked through something, finally recognizing the obstacles I'd put in front of him so he wouldn't see how messy my family was, that on the most basic level, we didn't function. My mother couldn't even walk. She was an infant in her forties.

"Ignore them," I said.

"It's Tom," Tom said. I admired Tom's response to my parents and appreciated his lack of pity. I once let Daniel's mother call me Suzy all day long, not wanting to upset her.

"I thought his name was Daniel," my father said.

"Dad," I said.

"Alan," my mother said.

"Just a joke. Daniel's her boyfriend. How quickly forgotten, off in Vietnam."

I hadn't told Tom about Daniel, either.

"Alan, butt out! Let the two of them go, already," my mother said.

"Daniel could be dead right now," Tom said. "Then the joke wouldn't be funny."

I thought for sure I'd feel better about Tom's comment than I did, but I left for the rally with a burn in my gut like I'd broken an oath. I imagined my parents back on the porch in the waning sun, bickering.

9

Heddon Hall gathered a crowd by the time Tom and I reached the President's House, a grand Victorian on the lawn of the building, the kind of house I'd always admired.

Next to a magnolia tree, a small group of protestors were already shouting, "Draft beer, not boys!" I wondered if they realized they were dealing with the President of Bridgeport University and not the President of the United States.

The students were flocked in white shirts, jeans and sneakers at the entrance to the building. I wanted to feel enraged, to have such a definition between what was right and wrong, so I tried imagining Daniel, maimed and pleading for help, but all I could picture was when he was safe at home in his button-up seersucker shirt and jean shorts.

The fliers had been everywhere for days, so the police and ambulances were expecting The Takeover, and some residents on Holmes Street stood outside their doors spectating like they did after major wind and ice storms.

"Just don't burn the place down," a man with his poodle said to Tom as they approached the building. The protestors on the lawn looked to Tom for some guidance and fell in line behind him. No wonder he wanted to be around me, I thought. I was someone wanting to be led.

One kid handed Tom a joint he passed on to me. "Boyfriend, huh?" he said, as though sharing with me was some sort of favor, given I hadn't told him about Daniel.

I smoked eagerly and heavily, waiting for something to hit me. I coughed from the burn I hadn't felt in so long. Before Daniel left, we would light up sometimes in the parking lot at night and find relief from talking about our parents by instead focusing on the paranoia of being caught.

I took the joint and sat against the lobby wall while Tom dished the plan to the protestors. We wouldn't leave for the whole night. The Heddon Takeover meant turning the administration building into our own space, where we would do whatever we liked.

It was the lightest I'd felt in months.

I crossed my feet at the ankles like the girl I was a year ago. I couldn't shout in protest without being embarrassed.

Tom kept one eye on me, propped against a pillar in the lobby, somewhere between tired and high.

"What do you expect the rally to produce?" a young administrator asked, appearing not much older than the oldest student.

"Exemption from final exams," Tom said.

I laughed loud. "Really?"

Tom kicked me lightly in the ankle with his bare toes. My jaw clenched.

I thought back to what Tom said to my father about Daniel, how he could be dead, and supposed I never really wondered what the end goal was of these protests. The posters never mentioned a thing about exams. I considered stomping on Tom's foot.

"We shouldn't continue our lives—academic or otherwise—when there are soldiers dying," a girl said. A long braid roped down her back and I wondered what she would look like without peace signs on her cheeks.

A man in a suit remarked to another he didn't think the kids were going to be violent. The suits and the students faced each other awkwardly and anticlimactically until one student yelled out, "Peace takes brains!" and the rest cheered.

Tom shouted with the others until administrators shrugged their shoulders and left, and I suddenly felt pity for him, so far away from the people he protested for, far away from death and still needing to act the part. How could he understand tragedy without understanding the people involved?

In the halls of the administration building, students smoked and played guitar and danced, and when they talked to me, I found myself nervously looking away, as though I were guilty of not caring enough to dance and have sex in the name of peace.

It was the same type of stare my mother gave me when I ignored her plea to adopt Baby Alice. There were reasons to embrace life and reasons to abandon it. My mother had no concept of either, which I realized that morning while watching her drag herself along the porch floor.

St. Barnabas had left a message on the Phone Mate the day before—I was to return to the home that week to sign the relinquishment papers so Baby Alice could be adopted. They had a nice Catholic family lined up, and all they needed was my signature. Until then, the nun said, my baby was in a sort of Purgatory, and did I want that?

There was splashing and laughing in the building pool, an odd addition to the administration building, where two protestors wrestled in the water and one swam laps determinedly. I wondered if this counted as going on with his life.

"Come on, June," Tom said. "Let's hop in."

He pulled his shirt up over his head, revealing rib after rib after rib. My body didn't resemble what it was before I had Alice. As a child, my mother used to push me off her lap, complaining about my bony butt. But now, I had an awkward softer figure on its way to resembling my mother's.

"I am not skinny dipping," I said. "Go by yourself."

Though Tom looked so helpless and skinny—and maybe *because* he looked so helpless and skinny—I wanted to go with him in the water. But I couldn't, I'd already said no. I wanted him to follow me when I left, which would be any minute. And when he wouldn't, I'd think about what a farce his protest was, and anger myself, and demonize Tom, and remember Daniel as a saint.

Tom stood in his jeans with his hands clasped on the top of his head.

"No taking care of your mom tonight, June," Tom said. "Have a beer and come in the water. Relax," he said. "Have a good time."

I thought back to my father that day: *Lighten up, Alice.*

"All in the name of protest, right?" I asked. I was making it worse, my life, and I shouldn't have come. I didn't need Tom to bring me to St. Barnabas tomorrow. I could call a cab. I didn't need a caretaker.

"Okay, fine. Maybe if you could see outside of *your* little world, you'd actually live *your* life," Tom said. "I'm done chasing you, June."

I knew this battle from the inside out. My stomach coiled. I placed my hands squarely on Tom's chest, and pushed, finally and with the might I'd held for so long. He fell backward, arms spread wide as he smacked the pool water. I turned away and walked.

The officers were shining flashlights at the bell tower when I stepped into the cool night, alone. There was a curly-haired meaty student scaling the ornate scrolls with a sheet tied around his neck as a cape, a peace sign painted on it in orange paint. The carillon bells signaled midnight.

The officers said something to me, but I kept walking. Tom was still in the building, probably still in the water, and would have to leave soon, I thought, if the police had anything to do with it.

If I were honest with myself, I would go back in Heddon Hall, to Tom, but I hated this part. I hated that cloying post-argument makeup, grinning at the other person every time they said two words so they wouldn't think you were still angry. I was still angry.

I stopped on the sidewalk of Holmes Street, and my view landed in Daniel's mother's living room. She was reading and held a tissue in her hand. Maybe she was crying over Daniel or maybe over a fight she had with her dead husband. Maybe she had a cold or was reading a sad book or was done with her laundry and her baking and realized she had nothing left to do and no one left to do it for.

When I thought of Tom, I was angry in the most satisfying way, how the crunch of a metal against metal could somehow relieve something inside you, or the sting of an injection could make you feel clean. He was living for lives he couldn't touch, propagandizing war for the sake of exam week. He shrank to me, skinny dipping in the Heddon pool, coaxing me in while Daniel was at war.

The last thing I wanted to do was go home to my mother. In my mother's mind, things were so simple: You either wanted something, and so you did it. Or you didn't want something, so you ignored it. But as time went on, over the past few weeks, my mother should have, might have, recognized that her offer to care for Baby Alice became less of an option, though she still talked about it as though it were possible.

"I'll clean out the landing upstairs," my mother said to me. "We'll put a crib up there." My father and I knew if *we* didn't do it, it wouldn't get done, which brought me the most despair of all.

The canal had been filled with water after the winter drain. Boats began to dock with the mild weather. At the Erie Ave bridge, a boat painted with a dead bird was parked against the canal's edge, and not far away, a couple dangled their feet against the scraggly bank, drinking beers and smoking cigarettes in the streetlights like my parents should have been. When I tried to imagine my parents' future, even as individuals, I couldn't.

When I tried to imagine Baby Alice at St. Barnabas, I couldn't. When I tried to place Daniel in the world anywhere, I couldn't. I could only know where I was, myself, alone in the blue-black night.

As though on autopilot, I ended up at my parents' house. The orange wheelchair was parked at the curb. There was little worse than having nowhere to go and plenty of time, and ending up, by default, in the same place you always went. My entire life, my parents showed me sacrifice and called what they had 'good' because it belonged to them.

When I entered, my father slept on the couch, a Genny on the coffee table and his shoes beneath. There were two empty coffee cups on the kitchen counter and two crummy plates in the sink. I washed my face, then found the number for a cab to St. Barnabas to sign the papers.

I pulled a chair over to my mother, who slept in her bed, mouth wide open, hair a mess. The sky dawned slowly, splaying lemon on the open window. I wrapped myself in Mom's homemade afghan, and feeling so, so, tired, closed my eyes in wait for her to wake up.

Acknowledgments

First, thank you to my husband, Cory Cedeño and sons, Johnny and Sammy, for love and support during the writing journey, which, early on, took me to Vermont for weeks at a time. To John and Sam, for spending hours at the museum while I read *Brockport Republic* articles and searched archives. To Cory, for being my ultimate first reader and for always supporting my goals. Thank you three for modeling the hard work and perseverance (on the ice and in the working world) that inspires me to keep going. I love you, love you, love you.

Thank you to my parents, John and Linda Lotze, for growing our large family with unconditional love and complexity of character, for encouraging and supporting me during my very lucrative degrees, and for moving to Spring Street. To Micheil, one of my first models of what it was to be a woman and who endured the years I was her shadow gracefully. To Jamie, who shares my curiosity of local history, the morbid, ghosts, and who frightened me with the prophecies of Nostradamus. And to Darrin, for driving me to Vermont, telling me upstate stories, and inspiring the buck scene in "You Hear Night Sounds."

Thank you to George and Myriam Cedeño for believing in my work and sharing it with friends and family and for unlimited childcare and support while I was at Goddard residencies or while I was here and working.

I'm indebted to the group at the Emily L. Knapp Museum & Library of Local History. Especially the late Jacklyn Morris, Village Historian, who had the arresting officers of the 1980s High Street murder over for tea after my inquiry and welcomed me back to the unofficial afternoon coffee club—I loved the chatty, hilarious, hours with the late Doug Wolcott, resident cynic Dan Burns, Rayleen Bucklin, and the always knowledgeable and energetic Sue Savard, devoted museum steward. Thanks to Historian and Professor Emerita Bill Andrews for meeting at Java Junction to chat about Joel Rifkin, his student at SUNY Brockport from 1978-1979. Thanks to Alicia Kerfoot, friend and kindred spirit, for digging through archives and imagining history with me. Thanks to Bill

Cowling, former SUNY Brockport archivist, who let me spend a day in the Rose Archives researching college history.

Thanks to Sarah Freligh for friendship and valuable writing advice, for connecting me to opportunities, supporting writers, and sharing wine. To creative writing colleagues and friends who nurtured me in my early writing days and continue to, Ralph Black, Jim Whorton, Steve Fellner, and Anne Panning. Thanks to Alicia Kerfoot, Janie Hinds, Denise Craft, MJ Iuppa, Kristen Proehl, and Carter Soles for your warmth, friendship, and inspiration.

So many thanks to those who volunteered to be first readers (though are also friends): David Corbin, Bill Pruitt, Elizabeth Cenci, Teri Whiting, Stacie Peck, Deborah Johnstone, Valerie Dimino, Brenda Beardsley, Kurt Hammel, and Barbara Purinton. Thanks, also, to those who've read stories from this collection at various times in their entirety or parts and offered valuable feedback: Robin Black, John McManus, Nicky Morris, Michael Klein, John Lotze, Aunt Hilary Larkin, Anne Panning, Jim Whorton, and Jennifer Heiner.

To Goddard College (RIP, 2024), for the space and time to write, for the bonfires, Mr. Jones, wall graffiti in the Music Room, for perpetual bacon and potato breakfasts, for all the kale. For the magical space where I met generous souls, thought-provoking writers, and made peace with the sensitive spirit I've been all along. Thanks to John McManus, who provided thoughtful, generative feedback during my thesis project. Learning from him had the biggest influence on me as a teacher.

Thank you to the SUNY Brockport Writers Forum for bringing diverse writers to its suburban campus, for modeling the connections writers can have with communities, and for privileging writing and conversations about humanity regardless of immediate economic value. May its legacy continue with the support it deserves.

Thanks to students who bring energy and inspiration to the writing classroom, who keep us learning by asking questions.

Huge thanks to *The Rumpus* for publishing "You Hear Nights Sounds" and to *New World Writing* for publishing "Orient Express."

Thanks to Megan Merchant for her evocative cover art, "I woke to the sound of rain" and to Diana Baltag for the bold cover design.

Thanks to Allison Blevins, Kristiane Weeks-Rogers, Bianca Dagostino, Claire Eder, Dustin Brookshire, and everyone at Small Harbor Publishing for taking on this project and seeing it to fruition. And for doing the good work of bringing words to the world. Go indie presses!

Sarah Cedeño's debut story collection, *The Grand Scheme of Things*, was published by *Harbor Editions* in July of 2025. Her collection of essays, *Not Something We Discuss Often*, was published by Harbor Editions in November 2022. Her essay "The Visible Woman" was selected by Vivian Gornick as a Notable Essay in *The Best American Essays 2022*. Her work has appeared in *Brevity, Salamander, The Journal, The Pinch, The Baltimore Review, Hippocampus Magazine, Bellevue Literary Review*, and elsewhere. Sarah holds an MFA from Goddard College. She lives in Brockport, NY with her husband, two sons, some old ghosts, and two German shepherds. She teaches writing at her alma mater, SUNY Brockport.

About Small Harbor Publishing

Small Harbor Publishing is a 501c3 nonprofit organization. Our goal is to publish unique and diverse voices. We are a feminist press, and we are committed to diversity and inclusion. We strive to bring new voices to a devoted and expanding readership.

Small Harbor Publishing began in 2018 with the first issue of *Harbor Review*. The magazine is an online space where poetry and art converse. *Harbor Review* quickly grew and now publishes reviews and runs multiple micro chapbook competitions, including the Washburn Prize and the Editor's Prize.

In July 2020, Small Harbor Publishing was officially incorporated and began Harbor Editions. Harbor Editions accepts submissions through a chapbook open reading period, a hybrid chapbook open reading period, the Marginalia Series, and the Laureate Prize.

In 2023, Harbor Anthologies began with a mission to promote texts that explore social justice issues and highlight marginalized writers.

If you would like to support Small Harbor Publishing, please visit our "About" page at smallharborpublishing.com/about.

www.ingramcontent.com/pod-product-compliance
Lightning Source LLC
Chambersburg PA
CBHW020203090426
42734CB00008B/928